T0004129

PRAYING YOUR WAY TO A HAPPY LIFE

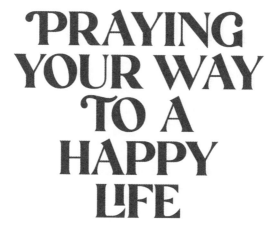

PRAYING YOUR WAY TO A HAPPY LIFE

Daily Inspiration for Women

BARBOUR
PUBLISHING

© 2023 by Barbour Publishing, Inc.

Print ISBN 987-1-63609-636-0

Text compiled from: *Praying Your Way to Forgiveness* by Bekah Jane Pogue, *Praying Your Way to Peace* by Donna K. Maltese, and *Praying Your Way to Joy* by Donna K. Maltese, © by Barbour Publishing, Inc. All rights reserved.

All rights reserved. No part of this publication may be reproduced or transmitted for commercial purposes, except for brief quotations in printed reviews, without written permission of the publisher. Reproduced text may not be used on the World Wide Web.

Churches and other noncommercial interests may reproduce portions of this book without the express written permission of Barbour Publishing, provided that the text does not exceed 500 words or 5 percent of the entire book, whichever is less, and that the text is not material quoted from another publisher. When reproducing text from this book, include the following credit line: "From *Praying Your Way to a Happy Life: Daily Inspiration for Women*, published by Barbour Publishing, Inc. Used by permission."

Scripture quotations marked AMPC are taken from the Amplified® Bible, Classic Edition © 1954, 1958, 1962, 1964, 1965, 1987 by The Lockman Foundation. Used by permission.

Scripture quotations marked NLV are taken from the New Life Version copyright © 1969 and 2003 by Barbour Publishing, Inc., Uhrichsville, Ohio, 44683. All rights reserved.

Scripture quotations marked NKJV are taken from the New King James Version®. Copyright © 1982 by Thomas Nelson, Inc. Used by permission. All rights reserved.

Scripture quotations marked ESV are from The Holy Bible, English Standard Version®, copyright © 2001 by Crossway Bibles, a publishing ministry of Good News Publishers. Used by permission. All rights reserved.

Scripture quotations marked NIV are taken from the HOLY BIBLE, NEW INTERNATIONAL VERSION®. NIV®. Copyright © 1973, 1978, 1984, 2011 by Biblica, Inc.™ Used by permission. All rights reserved worldwide.

Scripture quotations marked MSG are from *THE MESSAGE*. Copyright © by Eugene H. Peterson 1993, 1994, 1995, 1996, 2000, 2001, 2002. Used by permission of NavPress Publishing Group.

Scripture quotations marked HCSB are taken from the Holman Christian Standard Bible ® Copyright © 1999, 2000, 2002, 2003, 2009 by Holman Bible Publishers. Used with permission by Holman Bible Publishers, Nashville, Tennessee. All rights reserved.

Cover Design: Greg Jackson, Thinkpen Design

Published by Barbour Publishing, Inc., 1810 Barbour Drive, Uhrichsville, Ohio 44683, www.barbourbooks.com

Our mission is to inspire the world with the life-changing message of the Bible.

Member of the
Evangelical Christian
Publishers Association

Printed in China.

INTRODUCTION

*If you crave a life full of peace and joy. . .this book
of daily prayers is just what your heart needs!*

This book of daily inspirational prayers will put you on a
path to joy-filled living. Each devotional-like prayer and
related scripture selection will help you to discover true
delight and contentment, peace and comfort, compassion and
grace, and so much more, every day of the year! Between
the pages of this book, you'll encounter a life of purpose
with the heavenly Father as your friend and guide.

*A truly happy life...
is just a prayer away!*

A GLIMPSE OF A SMILE

A happy heart makes the face cheerful, but heartache crushes the spirit. The discerning heart seeks knowledge, but the mouth of a fool feeds on folly. All the days of the oppressed are wretched, but the cheerful heart has a continual feast.

PROVERBS 15:13–15 NIV

. . . .

I passed my reflection in the mirror, then a storefront window, then the car rearview mirror, each time noticing my smile. It was missing. In its place was a furrowed brow and focused scowl. How sad. How sad that when I catch a glimpse of my face, it's unsmiling.

God, please forgive me for being so focused on the next task that I forget to carry Your joy on my face. A smile is a free gift—a reminder that *all* of life is a gift. In the morning, Lord, will You please nudge me to first notice Your joy that fills me from the inside? Will You prompt me to dress my face with a smile—a genuine expression that reflects the deep knowledge that the Holy Spirit dwells within me? What do I have to fear? What is more important than this?

God, please continue to use my countenance to display that my soul and smile are from You. Amen.

Day 2

DIPPING INTO
GOD'S STRENGTH

*They read from the book of the Law of God, telling
the meaning of it so that they understood what was
read. . . . Ezra said to them, "Go, eat and drink what
you enjoy, and give some to him who has nothing
ready. For this day is holy to our Lord. Do not be
sad for the joy of the Lord is your strength."*
NEHEMIAH 8:8, 10 NLV

Lord, so many times I find myself trying to live in my own
strength, and by the end of the day I come up empty and
sad, tired and worn. Yet when I see this passage in Your
Book, I realize I've been drawing from the wrong well.
So here I am, Lord, coming to You, finding where my true
strength lies—in Your joy. I am dipping into Your love,
communing with Your Spirit, filling up on the sheer bliss of
Your presence. Be with me here and now and throughout
this day as I feast on You, share Your blessings with others,
and discover Your everlasting joy. Amen.

Day 3

LIVE CAREFREE

*All of you, leaders and followers alike, are to be down
to earth with each other, for—God has had it with the
proud, but takes delight in just plain people. So be content
with who you are, and don't put on airs. God's strong
hand is on you; he'll promote you at the right time.
Live carefree before God; he is most careful with you.*

1 PETER 5:5–7 MSG

. . . .

Lord, I want to be down-to-earth, talking straight not only
to other humans but to You too. But I'll need Your help.
Please give me the courage to tell You everything that's
happening in my life; the things I've thought, said, and
done; the good, the bad, and the ugly. I want not just to
be satisfied, content with who I am, but to be assured that
You too are content—perhaps even happy—with who I
am or the woman I'm working toward being. But most
of all, Lord, I want to turn over to You *all* the things that
are bothering me, give You *all* my burdens, my fumes and
frets, and leave them in Your more than capable hands.
In Jesus' name, amen.

Day 4

EVEN AT NIGHT

I will give honor and thanks to the Lord, Who has told me what to do. Yes, even at night my mind teaches me. I have placed the Lord always in front of me. Because He is at my right hand, I will not be moved. And so my heart is glad. My soul is full of joy. My body also will rest without fear.

PSALM 16:7–9 NLV

. . . .

You, Lord, are the font of wisdom. You are the one who knows all things—even how many hairs are on my head! So I am giving honor and thanks to You. Show me which way to go, what to say, when to say it. At night, Lord, stop all those what-if thoughts from ricocheting around in my head. Replace them with Your peace and presence. With You next to me, I know nothing can shake me. I can stand in confidence and move forward in hope. You make my heart soar with gladness. You fill my soul with joy. My body relaxes in Your all-encompassing peace as I lean back upon You and rest my weary head. Amen.

Day 5

FREE AND UNINHIBITED

*When the LORD restored the fortunes of Zion, we were like
those who dream. Then our mouth was filled with laughter,
and our tongue with shouts of joy; then they said among
the nations, "The LORD has done great things for them."
The LORD has done great things for us; we are glad.*
PSALM 126:1–3 ESV

. . . .

God, today I saw a little girl walk up to another girl at a
restaurant and introduce herself. "You wanna play?" she
asked innocently. I want to be that little girl again. Childlike
confidence. A willingness to laugh and play and befriend
perfect strangers. I admit, becoming an adult dulls the free
spirit inside, and I ask for Your forgiveness in dimming
the light You placed in me from birth.

Father, renew that little girl inside me. Invite me to
laugh until I snort and to play hard, without care for what
others think. Please quiet the lies that threaten to silence
a playful spirit and childlike faith. Bring to mind ways I
was most alive when I was younger, and invite me to live
free and uninhibited. May I resolve to journey toward joy
and leave laughter in my wake. Amen.

Day 6

DOS AND DON'TS

Bless your enemies; no cursing under your breath.
Laugh with your happy friends when they're happy;
share tears when they're down. Get along with each
other; don't be stuck-up. Make friends with nobodies;
don't be the great somebody. Don't hit back; discover
beauty in everyone. If you've got it in you, get along
with everybody. Don't insist on getting even; that's
not for you to do. "I'll do the judging," says God.
ROMANS 12:14–19 MSG

. . . .

Even though I myself am included in "people," Lord, I do not understand why people do what they do. Yet You would have me love them and live at peace with them whether I understand them or not. So please give me the strength to bless people who work against me. At the same time, give me the heart to laugh with my friends when they're happy and to cry with them when they're sad. Show me the way to stay humble. And above all, Lord, help me to find something beautiful in every person I meet, to see the good within and not the bad. To look to make peace and live in love with all, in Jesus' name. Amen.

Day 7

ALL GOOD THINGS

Keep me, O God, for I am safe in You. I said to the Lord, "You are my Lord. All the good things I have come from You." As for those in the land who belong to You, they are the great ones in whom is all my joy.
PSALM 16:1–3 NLV

. . . .

Lord, when I am alone, scared, or confused, I know I can run to You. You are the one who can protect me from all that comes against me, within and without. In You I can hide from the lure of the world. In You my soul and spirit find peace and calm. You have a way of unruffling my feathers, ever so gently. So now, in this moment, I come to rest in Your companionable light, love, and silence. Place Your hedge of protection around me, sheltering me from outside dangers and inner negative thoughts. Remind me that all the good I have in this life comes from You. Thank You, Lord, for all Your blessings upon me and for all the joy You have waiting for me as I wait on You. "You are my Lord. All the good things I have come from You." In Jesus' name I pray, amen.

Day 8

TRUSTING CONFIDENCE

Thus said the Lord God, the Holy One of Israel:
In returning [to Me] and resting [in Me] you shall be saved;
in quietness and in [trusting] confidence shall be your
strength. . . . And your ears will hear a word behind
you, saying, This is the way; walk in it, when you turn
to the right hand and when you turn to the left.

ISAIAH 30:15, 21 AMPC

. . . .

These words are a reminder to me, Lord, of what I need to do, what I *want* to do, to have a good and peaceable life. I'm to return to You, to depend on You alone—not on fellow humans, animals, or machines. Only then will I find the true rest I need each day. Only then will my spirit find the quietness that feeds it, my soul the trusting confidence that nourishes it. As I rest and replenish myself in You, I find the strength to do what You've created me to do, to be who You created me to be. As I walk, Lord, direct my feet. Open my ears to Your Spirit's guidance every step of the way. Amen.

Day 9

HAPPINESS FOREVER

My future is in Your hands. The land given to me is good. Yes, my share is beautiful to me. . . . For You will not give me over to the grave. And You will not allow Your Holy One to return to dust. You will show me the way of life. Being with You is to be full of joy. In Your right hand there is happiness forever.

PSALM 16:5–6, 10–11 NLV

. . . .

Lord, when I'm stuck in a pattern of negative thoughts or am allowing fear to control my life, my heart races, my brow sweats, my soul despairs, and my spirit sinks. And it's all because I've somehow moved away from You. I've forgotten Your power, grace, mercy, strength, and help. I'm allowing everything *but You* to control me. So I'm back, Lord, remembering *You* are the one who holds my future. *You* are the one who helped me in the past and have given me all the good I have. So here I am in the present in Your presence. Here with You, I find my joy! For I know You will show me the way You would have me go, the way that leads to that happily forever after. Amen.

Day 10

THANKS IN THE EVERYDAY-NESS

*Whatever you do, work at it with all your heart,
as working for the Lord, not for human masters,
since you know that you will receive an inheritance from
the Lord as a reward. It is the Lord Christ you are serving.*
Colossians 3:23–24 NIV

God, I admit, as I'm washing dishes, that I forget to thank You for the everyday provisions like plates and forks and food. How much I have to be thankful for and how often I neglect to pause and thank You first for the miraculously minuscule ways You show up—in weekday dinners and dirty silverware. These reminders are Your invitation for community, eating with neighbors, and enjoying recipes together. The dish washing is the celebration for a meal well spent, conversations well shared. Plates and forks joyfully messied. Forgive me for complaining instead of rejoicing. Turn my heart now toward praise. Yay for dirty dishes, for each one signifies a person fed nourishment and soul care in my home. May You be the center of every meal and conversation from this day forward.

Day 11

GOD IS NEAR

Rejoice in the Lord always [delight, gladden yourselves in Him]; again I say, Rejoice! Let all men know and perceive and recognize your unselfishness (your considerateness, your forbearing spirit). The Lord is near [He is coming soon]. Do not fret or have any anxiety about anything, but in every circumstance and in everything, by prayer and petition (definite requests), with thanksgiving, continue to make your wants known to God. And God's peace [shall be yours].
PHILIPPIANS 4:4–7 AMPC

. . . .

More often than not, Lord, I find myself complaining about my lot in life, how hard it is just to survive sometimes. But moaning and groaning just bring me down even further. So I'm making it a point, Lord, to memorize and live these verses. To rejoice because You are with me. To let others see how gentle I am in You. To show them—and perhaps myself—that I know I never need to worry or complain because You are with me. Because You are so near, as near as my next breath, I need not be anxious. Instead, I will pray to You, ask for what I need, and count on You to listen and provide. For then, and only then, will I have the peace I require and desire. Amen.

Day 12

KEEP ASKING, SEEKING, AND KNOCKING

*Keep on asking and it will be given you;
keep on seeking and you will find; keep on knocking
[reverently] and [the door] will be opened to you.
For everyone who keeps on asking receives;
and he who keeps on seeking finds; and to him
who keeps on knocking, [the door] will be opened.*
MATTHEW 7:7–8 AMPC

. . . .

Just when I'm ready to give up, Lord, You bring scriptures like this to my attention and give me the hope I need to keep coming to You. Through Your Son, Jesus, You've made it clear that if I keep asking, seeking, and knocking, You *will* come through for me. I *will* receive what I'm asking for, find what I seek, and have doors opened to me. So here I am, Lord, asking, seeking, and knocking, knowing You will provide what I desire. And that, if need be, You'll change that desire to better align with Yours. In this and so many other ways, Lord, You revive my hope. Joy begins to warm my heart as my discouragement morphs into encouragement. Thank You for all this and more. I pray in Jesus' name, amen.

Day 13

STRONG AND COURAGEOUS

"No one will be able to stand against you as long as you live. I will be with you, just as I was with Moses. I will not leave you or forsake you. Be strong and courageous. . . . Above all, be strong and very courageous to carefully observe the whole instruction My servant Moses commanded you. Do not turn from it to the right or the left, so that you will have success wherever you go."
JOSHUA 1:5–7 HCSB

. . . .

When I hear or read words such as these, Lord, I realize I need not let my fears overwhelm me or even disturb me. Instead I'm to remember, believe, and trust Your Word is truth and power. Because You are with me, no one can stand against me. Just as You were with Moses and Joshua, You are also with me, here and now. So today, as I take up Your courage, my fears are banished. Your peace now reigns in their place. Unencumbered by worries and woes, I can finally breathe, stand firm, and walk where You would have me walk. In Jesus' name, amen.

Day 14

GIVING WAY TO GOD

*Do not trouble yourself because of sinful men. Do not
want to be like those who do wrong. For they will soon
dry up like the grass. Like the green plant they will
soon die. Trust in the Lord, and do good. So you will live
in the land and will be fed. Be happy in the Lord.
And He will give you the desires of your heart. Give your
way over to the Lord. Trust in Him also. And He will do it.*
PSALM 37:1–5 NLV

Lord, through Your Word, You have given me the way to
walk the road of joy. First, I'm not to worry about those
who are divisive or seem intent on doing evil. They will
not be around forever. Instead, I'm to trust in You and
do good in this world. Then I will find all I need to live
the life You have designed for me. Then I will find all the
joy in You and receive the desires of my heart. So in this
moment, right here, right now, I'm letting You take control
of my life. I'm trusting You for all, knowing it is in You
alone I'll find joy. Amen.

Day 15

ALREADY ENDOWED

The angel of G*OD* *appeared to him and said, "*G*OD* *is*
with you, O mighty warrior!" Gideon replied,
"With me, my master? If G*OD* *is with us, why has all*
this happened to us? . . . The fact is, G*OD* *has nothing to*
do with us—he has turned us over to Midian." But G*OD*
faced him directly: "Go in this strength that is yours."
J*UDGES* 6:12–14 MSG

. . . .

Some days, Lord, I'm so discouraged. So many things are
happening in this world that are beyond my control. So
many things are keeping me up at night, as I wonder and
worry about what may happen next. So many things seem
to be so much bigger than me and my faith. So many things
going wrong make me wonder where You are.

And then You appear in my mind. You whisper in my
ear. You remind me that because You are with me, I will
never be alone. You tell me to move forward in the strength
You have spoken into my life, the strength that is now part
of me, owned by me.

You alone give me peace and respite from the world's
troubles, Lord. You alone are bigger than anything that
can ever come against me. Help me, Lord, to take on the
power, to assume the mantle of strength with which You've
endowed me. In Jesus' name, amen.

Day 16

THE SHEER BEAUTY
OF CREATING

*"He has filled them with skill to do all kinds of
work as engravers, designers, embroiderers in blue,
purple and scarlet yarn and fine linen, and weavers—
all of them skilled workers and designers."*

EXODUS 35:35 NIV

. . . .

I am made in the image of the mighty Creator and therefore
am creative. God, awaken me to ways that You made me
to feel alive while creating. Is it picking wildflowers and
pressing them between book pages to make art? Is it baking
cookies for the neighborhood kids? Is it singing? Writing?
Quilting? Whatever the creative magic You sewed into me
since before time, pull that out of me today. Help me delight
in creating for the sheer beauty of creating—not the final
result, but the joy in the creative process. Forgive me when
I forget that this spark You've given me is unique; no one
else has the same way of creating from my perspective.
Help me not squander but generously use my gift. I'm so
thankful I have a Father who enjoys making and creating
and living alive in this creative space. Amen.

Day 17

A PICTURE OF PEACE

*Like an apple tree among the trees of the wood,
so is my beloved [shepherd] among the sons [cried
the girl]! . . . [I can feel] his left hand under my head
and his right hand embraces me! . . . [Vividly she
pictured it] The voice of my beloved [shepherd]! . . .
Arise, my love, my fair one, and come away.*
SONG OF SOLOMON 2:3, 6, 8, 13 AMPC

. . . .

You, Lord, are my pathway to peace. I look to You. I picture
You lying beside me. When I close my eyes and imagine You here with me, I can feel Your left hand under
my head, Your right hand embracing me, pulling me close
to Your warmth and love, giving me the comfort I long
for. And as I lie here, totally content, amazingly calm, I
know nothing can harm me. Nothing can worry or dismay
me. For I not only feel Your presence but hear Your voice
telling me You love me. That You will continually protect
and guide me. That because of You in my life, I need not
complain, worry, or fear. Thank You, Lord, for this picture
of peace. Amen.

Day 18

GREAT EXPECTATIONS

*The Lord [earnestly] waits [expecting, looking,
and longing] to be gracious to you; and therefore
He lifts Himself up, that He may have mercy on you
and show loving-kindness to you. . . . Blessed (happy,
fortunate, to be envied) are all those who [earnestly]
wait for Him, who expect and look and long for Him
[for His victory, His favor, His love, His peace,
His joy, and His matchless, unbroken companionship]!*
ISAIAH 30:18 AMPC

How wonderful, Lord, that in every moment You are waiting and expecting to be gracious to me. You have scads of mercy and loving-kindness whenever I need it. So help me be patient, Lord. Help me to drop whatever burdens I'm bearing and open up my arms to You and the blessings You have for me. My eyes are on You. I long for Your neverending supply of strength, love, peace, and joy. I cherish and seek out Your company, Your "matchless, unbroken companionship" each and every second of my day. For I know that by returning and resting in You, I will be saved. In quietness and trusting confidence I will find my source of strength (see Isaiah 30:15). Amen.

MY BELOVED SHEPHERD

*[So I went with him, and when we were climbing
the rocky steps up the hillside, my beloved shepherd
said to me] O my dove, [while you are here]. . .in the
sheltered and secret place of the cliff, let me see your
face, let me hear your voice; for your voice is sweet,
and your face is lovely. [My heart was touched and I
fervently sang to him my desire] Take for us the foxes,
the little foxes that spoil the vineyards [of our love].*
SONG OF SOLOMON 2:14–15 AMPC

. . . .

In Your company, my beloved, I can climb to the highest
of heights. You keep me safe and secluded in Your secret
place. It's here You ask me to let You see my face and hear
my voice. Just the fact that You'd like to do those things, to
listen to me and love me, brings me so much joy. So I am
ready to raise my voice to You in song, Lord. Allow me to
stay in You, walk with You, climb with You. And to rest in
You, confident You will remove anything that threatens to
come between us. In Jesus' name, amen.

Day 20

BOLDLY BELIEVING

*If you don't know what you're doing, pray to the
Father. He loves to help. You'll get his help, and won't
be condescended to when you ask for it. Ask boldly,
believingly, without a second thought. People who
"worry their prayers" are like wind-whipped waves.
Don't think you're going to get anything from the Master
that way, adrift at sea, keeping all your options open.*
JAMES 1:5–8 MSG

Lord, I feel as if I'm sinking in a quagmire of confusion.
I don't know what to do, where to go, what to say, how to
proceed. Lord, help me. Show me the way to go, the path
to take, the words to say. I come to You boldly, with no
reservations. For I truly believe You want to help and will
choose the best path for me. And I'm not going to worry
about the answer You give me, wondering how this will
all work out. Instead, I am going to do whatever You call
me to do, knowing that whenever You're involved in my
plans, You will give me what I need to see them through
and lead me to a place of joy in the process. So tell me
what to do, Lord. Speak. Your servant is listening. Amen.

Day 21
FULL PLAY

*Consider it wholly joyful, my brethren, whenever you are
enveloped in or encounter trials of any sort or fall into
various temptations. Be assured and understand that
the trial and proving of your faith bring out endurance
and steadfastness and patience. But let endurance and
steadfastness and patience have full play and do a
thorough work, so that you may be [people] perfectly and
fully developed [with no defects], lacking in nothing.*
JAMES 1:2–4 AMPC

This is the joy I'd like to develop, Lord—joy that I can have
even in the midst of trials, troubles, and temptations. Help
me understand that everything I go through will make me
stronger in my faith and increase my patience, endurance,
and constancy in You. I realize all this comes to me so that
I might be fully developed, strong, totally complete, and
lacking nothing. Yet still, it can be difficult. So please, Lord,
give me Your grace and love, Your blessings and peace as
I continue on. Help me fully realize Your presence so that
I can find Your joy in each and every situation. In Jesus'
name, amen.

Day 22

THE BEAUTY OF A SUNSET

The whole earth is filled with awe at your wonders;
where morning dawns, where evening
fades, you call forth songs of joy.
PSALM 65:8 NIV

. . . .

God, I'm sitting on the porch, watching the sunset, and I'm in absolute awe of Your gifts of color—the way the apricot hues merge with stormy violets and the sunshine creates cloud outlines in the sky. How I love watching the sun set! As I do, I'm reminded that it's the close of the day.

How did I hear You today? Where did I see You? How were You wooing me to Your Spirit? What sounds and sights did You use to speak directly to my soul? What colors invited me to pause and take notice?

Who am I that You are aware and mindful of me? Yet, I'm so thankful You are. As I rock on this porch, I'm enraptured with Your creative beauty. I'm closing my eyes and saving this moment in my memory bank—a sky painting delivered from my heavenly Father, a one-of-a-kind piece of art. Amen.

A GREAT AND WONDERFUL CALM

They. . .awakened Him, saying, Lord, rescue and preserve us! We are perishing! And He said to them, Why are you timid and afraid, O you of little faith? Then He got up and rebuked the winds and the sea, and there was a great and wonderful calm (a perfect peaceableness). And the men were stunned with bewildered wonder and marveled, saying, What kind of Man is this, that even the winds and the sea obey Him!
MATTHEW 8:25–27 AMPC

. . . .

When I'm in the middle of a storm, Lord, I know that because of Your presence, because You are riding out the storm with me, I have nothing at all to worry about. I have nothing at all to fear. After all, You have already rescued me from death. You have already overcome all evil. So all I need to do is remain confident that You are in control of the situation. That You will, at just the right moment, rise up and tame the wind and waves assailing me. That You will take this tumultuous situation and bring into it a great and wonderful calm. And I will once more stand before You and marvel. Amen.

Day 24

MORE THAN YOU NEED

*Do not trouble yourself when all goes well with the
one who carries out his sinful plans. Stop being
angry. Turn away from fighting. Do not trouble
yourself. It leads only to wrong-doing. For those
who do wrong will be cut off. But those who wait for
the Lord will be given the earth. . . . And they will
be happy and have much more than they need.*

PSALM 37:7–9, 11 NLV

Sometimes, Lord, I get so discouraged. It seems as if the people who get all the breaks are those who are *not* followers of You! It's so frustrating. But then I remember that even those who seem to have everything actually have nothing—because they don't have You. So I'm not going to worry about the ne'er-do-wells. Instead, I'm going to focus my eyes on You. I'm going to do good because I know it not only pleases You but also gives me so much joy. I'm waiting on You, Lord, following You, loving You, looking to You for everything. For when I give You my all, I get Your all. Amen.

Day 25

A NEW SONG

Praise the Lord! Sing to the Lord a new song. . . !
Let Israel rejoice in Him, their Maker; let Zion's children
triumph and be joyful in their King! . . . For the Lord
takes pleasure in His people; He will beautify the humble
with salvation and adorn the wretched with victory.
Let the saints be joyful in the glory and beauty [which God
confers upon them]; let them sing for joy upon their beds.
Psalm 149:1–2, 4–5 ampc

. . . .

Once again, Lord, I cannot help but be amazed that You
take pleasure in my company! That You actually love when
I come into Your presence, knowing that I'm by no means
perfect yet overlooking that, because You see me through
the light and love of Jesus! This fills me with joy, Lord! It
makes me so happy that You long to adorn me with beauty
and glory. That where I see myself as weak, You see me full
of strength. That where I see myself as lacking, You see me
as having it all. Help me to see me as You see me, Lord, so
that I will have the confidence to do what You would have
me do and to be the joy-filled woman You designed me to
be. Amen!

Day 26

A SAFE PLACE

*The steps of a good man are led by the Lord. And He
is happy in his way. When he falls, he will not be
thrown down, because the Lord holds his hand. . . .
For the Lord loves what is fair and right. He does
not leave the people alone who belong to Him. . . .
He. . .saves them, because they go to Him for a safe place.*

PSALM 37:23–24, 28, 40 NLV

• •

Here's one of the things I love most about You, Lord. When
I follow Your way instead of my own, I am happy, full of
that inner joy only You can supply, no matter what happens.
Because even if I trip up, You come to my rescue. You hold
my hand and pull me back up on my feet so I can start
all over again. As I grow closer and closer to You, I know
I'm exactly where I belong. For You promise to always
be with me. You will never leave me alone because I am
Your daughter, precious in Your sight. And when things
go dark, when shadows chase me, I run to You—straight
into Your arms—where I am not only safe but comforted
and remade. Amen.

Day 27

"ALL IS WELL"

The child sat on her lap till noon, and then he died.
And she went up and laid him on the bed of the man of
God and shut the door behind him and went out. . . .
She said, "All is well." . . . When the man of God
saw her coming, he said to Gehazi his servant. . .
"Run at once to meet her and say to her, 'Is all well
with you? Is all well with your husband? Is all well
with the child?'" And she answered, "All is well."
2 KINGS 4:20–21, 23, 25–26 ESV

. . . .

There is something wonderful as well as disturbing in the story of the Shunammite woman, Lord. Even after her son dies, she keeps saying, "All is well." It's wonderful that she can remain that calm during such a heart-wrenching account. Yet at the same time, it's a bit disturbing that she does. What cool! What calm! Yet that's just the kind of peace I want, Lord. So help me to remember that with You living with me and in me, I too can have this woman's confidence. I too can have peace within even when it seems as if all is falling apart without. In Jesus' name, amen.

Day 28

BEAUTY ALL AROUND

"Consider how the wild flowers grow. They do not labor or spin. Yet I tell you, not even Solomon in all his splendor was dressed like one of these."
LUKE 12:27 NIV

God, I look outside and see the vibrant green of grass and yellow flashes of wildflowers. Your beauty is everywhere, waiting to be enjoyed. Every delicate flower, the blue of the sky, the way the clouds form shapes and wisp across the horizon. . . Draw me to notice Your beauty in every person I interact with, the cup I drink from, and the architecture of buildings.

You waste nothing in design and structure and nature. Even when I cut an apple horizontally, there is Your beauty staring back in the form of a star. I'm aware of how often I take Your beauty for granted, for all of this—the beach, culture, various dialects, people, forests, and waves—is merely a facet of Your beauty.

God, how I want the earth's beauty to be an overarching imitation of the beauty You are. How I long to be in Your presence one day and behold Your infinite beauty. Amen.

Day 29

TIMES TESTED

Dear friends, your faith is going to be tested as if it were going through fire. Do not be surprised at this. Be happy that you are able to share some of the suffering of Christ. When His shining-greatness is shown, you will be filled with much joy. If men speak bad of you because you are a Christian, you will be happy because the Spirit of shining-greatness and of God is in you.

1 PETER 4:12–14 NLV

These days, Lord, many people don't see the virtue of goodness, of following You. In fact, being a Christian seems to have a new connotation—and it's not deemed very positively at all! Your people are being tested, Lord. And amid these tests, I need Your power. I need Your strength to face those who malign me—and You! Help me not to be discouraged but to be encouraged, knowing that Jesus suffered too. He also was shamed and abused. And He came out smelling like a rose on the other side. Help me to do the same, Lord. To keep the joy of You in my heart and mind as You reside within me every step of the way! Amen.

Day 30

A GRAND PLAN

*I know the thoughts and plans that I have for you,
says the Lord, thoughts and plans for welfare and peace
and not for evil, to give you hope in your final outcome.
Then you will call upon Me, and you will come and pray
to Me, and I will hear and heed you. Then you will seek
Me, inquire for, and require Me [as a vital necessity] and
find Me when you search for Me with all your heart.*

JEREMIAH 29:11–13 AMPC

I love that You have a plan for me, Lord. The fact that You even *think* of me is astounding! Sometimes I feel so lost in this world, as if I'm just one more bit of dust, unimportant, overlooked. And then I read in Your Word that if I call on You, You will bend Your ear to my lips. You'll actually *listen* to me, hear what I have to say, and move to work in my life. If I seek You with my whole self—my heart, soul, mind, and strength—and need You in every way, I *will* find You. All this is a balm for my soul and a joy to my spirit. Amen.

Day 31

OPENED EYES

An army with horses and chariots was around the city.
Elisha's servant said to him, Alas, my master! What shall
we do? [Elisha] answered, Fear not; for those with us are
more than those with them. Then Elisha prayed, Lord,
I pray You, open his eyes that he may see. And the Lord
opened the young man's eyes, and he saw, and behold,
the mountain was full of horses and chariots of fire.
2 KINGS 6:15–17 AMPC

. . . .

Lord, I feel like I'm surrounded by chaos. I'm overwhelmed, feeling hemmed in, as if there's no way out. That I have done all that I can do. But this is a battle I can no longer fight. So it is to You that I turn for help, for a solution, for hope. And as I turn my thoughts to You, as I lay my problem at Your feet, I hear Your voice, Your words telling me not to fear. You are more than able to protect me from all things, all people—even from my own self, doubts, and negative thoughts. You alone make it clear that I need never worry because there is no force more powerful than You. With opened eyes, I find my joy, my peace, my renewed hope and vision in You. Amen!

Day 32

THE SECRET PLACE

The Lord is my light and the One Who saves me.
Whom should I fear? The Lord is the strength of my life.
Of whom should I be afraid? . . . In the day of trouble. . .
In the secret place. . .He will hide me. He will set
me high upon a rock. Then my head will be lifted up
above all those around me who hate me. I will give
gifts in His holy tent with a loud voice of joy.
PSALM 27:1, 5–6 NLV

Fear can be a major killjoy, but I'm shoring up my confidence in You, Lord. You are the most powerful being in heaven and on earth. So I need not fear anything or anyone who comes against me. You, Lord, are the one who gives me the strength to stand. My faith in You gives me the confidence I need. When the trouble starts, You give me shelter. You keep me from the darkness and warm me with Your light. When I'm in Your secret place, You increase my courage. And it is there that I cry out with joy, praising You with all my heart. Thank You, Lord, for being my all in all. Amen.

Day 33

RADIANT LIGHT

Then you shall see and be radiant, and your heart shall thrill and tremble with joy [at the glorious deliverance] and be enlarged. . . . The sun shall no more be your light by day, nor for brightness shall the moon give light to you, but the Lord shall be to you an everlasting light, and your God your glory and your beauty. Your sun shall no more go down, nor shall your moon withdraw itself, for the Lord shall be your everlasting light, and the days of your mourning shall be ended.
Isaiah 60:5, 19–20 AMPC

. . . .

How wonderful, Lord, that someday this world will be different. That I shall have the peace, joy, and honor that You have promised. That I'll no longer need the light of the sun or of the moon. For I'll be walking in *Your* light, day and night. I'll witness Your glory and Your beauty. And sorrow will be no more. What comfort and joy that brings me today, Lord, knowing that someday tears will no longer flow. Thank You, Father God, for the promise of this day. I tremble with joy in anticipation of what You have in store for those who love You. In Jesus' name, amen.

Day 34

A SPARK OF FUN
AND LAUGHTER

*So, whether you eat or drink, or whatever
you do, do all to the glory of God.*
1 CORINTHIANS 10:31 ESV

God, I could use some fun in my life. Some laughter and joy and a spark of hope. What is clouding the joy and stealing the celebration of today? Help me stay here long enough to ponder the deeper places of my heart and pull out the melancholy parts.

You don't ask me to get rid of my authentic emotions or stitch on a fake smile. You desire true life to bubble out of me, and I desperately want that. Please nudge me toward what will bring a sense of fun today. A nature walk? Baking? Going out with a friend? Tackling a creative project?

You know me best. I bring my bad attitude to You now and thank You for welcoming all of me. Invite me to note the spark of fun You long to join me in, and give me tenacity to embrace it with passion and curiosity. For You are a Father who is fun and loves to delight in Your daughter. Amen.

Day 35

BECAUSE OF YOU

Standing behind Him at His feet weeping, she began to
wet His feet with [her] tears; and she wiped them with
the hair of her head and kissed His feet [affectionately]
and anointed them with the ointment (perfume). . . .
He said to her, Your sins are forgiven! . . . Your faith has
saved you; go (enter) into peace [in freedom from all the
distresses that are experienced as the result of sin].
LUKE 7:38, 48, 50 AMPC

Jesus, You know I'm not perfect. Yet You still accept me, love me, help me, and understand me when I come before You. If I could, I would fall at Your feet, wet them with my tears of joy, wipe them with my hair, anoint them with perfume, and cover them in kisses. For because of You and what You did on the cross, my sins have been forgiven and forgotten. Because of You, I can come boldly before Father God and speak to Him. Because of You, I can have peace of mind and freedom from stress. Because of You, I have a life I want to live and yet surrender to You. What a God I serve! Amen!

Day 36

HEART STRONG

You have been my Helper. . . . For my father and
my mother have left me. But the Lord will take care
of me. . . . I would have been without hope if I had not
believed that I would see the loving-kindness of the Lord
in the land of the living. Wait for the Lord. Be strong.
Let your heart be strong. Yes, wait for the Lord.
PSALM 27:9–10, 13–14 NLV

Sometimes even when I'm surrounded by lots of people, I can feel all alone. I am out of step with them because I'm so in step with You, Lord. Yet strangely enough, it's in those times that I feel even closer to You. Because I know that no matter who I lose, I'll always have You. You are the helper I crave to be with. You are the one who has taken care of me in the past, is doing so in the present, and will continue to do so in the future. This gives me hope and revives my joy. For I know I'll see Your loving-kindness here and now. Meanwhile, I wait, knowing that as I do, You are keeping my heart and spirit strong. Amen.

Day 37

IN A NUTSHELL

Rejoice in the Lord always. . . . Let your reasonableness
be known to everyone. The Lord is at hand; do not be
anxious about anything, but in everything by prayer
and supplication with thanksgiving let your requests
be made known to God. And the peace of God, which
surpasses all understanding, will guard your hearts and
your minds in Christ Jesus. Finally. . .if there is anything
worthy of praise, think about these things. What you have
learned and received and heard and seen in me—practice
these things, and the God of peace will be with you.
PHILIPPIANS 4:4–9 ESV

. . . .

You, Lord, are the answer to my problem. As they have
before and will continue to do, Your words provide the
remedy to my wretchedness. Looking from my pain to Your
pleasure, I raise my thoughts to You and in praise of You.
Because You are so close, I need to fear nothing. Instead,
I bring my silent thank-Yous and pleas to You alone, heart
to heart. As I do, I am infused with Your peace. My mind
reels in all good things and casts out the not-so-good things.
I watch, listen, learn, and practice from the saints before
me. In a nutshell, I abide in You. Amen!

Day 38

REQUEST GRANTED

Jabez was honorable above his brothers; but his mother named him Jabez [sorrow maker], saying, Because I bore him in pain. Jabez cried to the God of Israel, saying, Oh, that You would bless me and enlarge my border, and that Your hand might be with me, and You would keep me from evil so it might not hurt me! And God granted his request.
1 CHRONICLES 4:9–10 AMPC

I thank You, Lord, that You have provided me with the gift and tool of prayer. No matter how I am seen or labeled in this world, by praying to You, I can change the conversation, within and without. Although my name is not Sorrow Maker, I ask You, Lord, for Your many blessings. I ask that You would increase what I already have. That Your hand would be with me to protect me. That You would keep me from evil so I am not hurt. That You would fill my head with good thoughts. That You would open my mind and heart to Your Word, allowing it to change me from the inside out for Your glory alone. In Jesus' name I pray, amen.

THE SOUL CHILD WITHIN

Lord, my heart is not haughty, nor my eyes lofty; neither do I exercise myself in matters too great or in things too wonderful for me. Surely I have calmed and quieted my soul; like a weaned child with his mother, like a weaned child is my soul within me [ceased from fretting]. O Israel, hope in the Lord from this time forth and forever.

PSALM 131:1–3 AMPC

. . . .

Father God, I have put aside any grandiose plans I may have had for myself. I don't get caught up in things that are way beyond my comprehension. Instead, I have put myself and my future in Your hands. I tackle the things You call me to do, follow the plans You have made for me, walk on the path You have laid out for me. I live and breathe in Your rhythm. In doing so, I have transformed my heart within to be calm. No outside or inside noises can shake me. I no longer fuss, fear, or fret. My soul is like a weaned child within me. I am in Your hands, held close with love because of Your Son, in whose name I pray. Amen.

Day 40

A STIR TO EXPERIENCE

"And I will ask the Father, and he will give you another advocate to help you and be with you forever—the Spirit of truth. The world cannot accept him, because it neither sees him nor knows him. But you know him, for he lives with you and will be in you."

JOHN 14:16–17 NIV

. . . .

Lord, I'm becoming aware of how I enter conversations and circumstances for what I will take *from* them, instead of simply experiencing. Forgive me for my focus on self-benefit, instead of on the sheer joy of being and sitting in awe of a new friendship, a conversation, a beautiful moment.

I confess my rushed mindset and ask You to transform my anxiousness to achieve. In its place, please stir me to experience. Experience You. Experience a new way I'm alive. Experience a new perspective. Experience the quiet. Experience fresh colors, smells, sounds, and textures.

What is life if not experienced? What is faith if not known? What is having access to a relationship with You if not noticed? Experience is my prayer. You are who I want to meet at every turn today. Amen.

Day 41

SPREADING THE WORD

Christ Who is Life was shown to us. We saw Him.
We tell you and preach about the Life that lasts forever.
He was with the Father and He has come down to us.
We are preaching what we have heard and seen.
We want you to share together with us what we
have with the Father and with His Son, Jesus Christ.
We are writing this to you so our joy may be full.
1 JOHN 1:2–4 NLV

* *

I can't imagine, Jesus, what it might have been like for Your followers to actually see, touch, and hear You. They could watch You, walk right beside You, or eat dinner with You. Yet what's even more amazing is that You and Your name live on. You knew people would be coming to You thousands of years after You passed into heaven. You made a way for me to follow You. And others wrote about You so that I could find my way and have the joy they had when they saw You face-to-face! I thank You, Jesus, for breathing Your Spirit into others so they would be inspired to spread not just Your Word but the joy of being in You. In Your name I pray, amen.

Day 42

"ALL IS WELL"

She went up and laid [her dead son] on the bed of the man
of God and shut the door behind him and went out. . . .
She said, "All is well." . . . She set out and came to the man
of God. . . . He said to Gehazi his servant, "Look, there is
the Shunammite. Run at once to meet her and say to her,
'Is all well with you? Is all well with your husband? Is all
well with the child?' " And she answered, "All is well."

2 KINGS 4:21, 23–26 ESV

. . . .

Lord, You Yourself know there is nothing harder in life
than losing one's only child. It is heartbreaking. Yet the
Shunammite woman had so much faith that even when
her child stopped breathing, she knew all would be well.
She set her face toward the man of God named Elisha,
knowing that through him, You would make everything all
right. And You did, bringing her child back to life! Help me,
Lord, to have the same attitude no matter what happens
in my life, no matter how You answer my prayers. Help
me live in and with peace and joy, knowing that with You,
all is and will be well. In Jesus' name, amen.

Day 43

A WAY FOLLOWER

"Blessed be GOD, who has given peace to his people Israel just as he said he'd do. Not one of all those good and wonderful words that he spoke through Moses has misfired. May GOD, our very own God, continue to be with us just as he was with our ancestors—may he never give up and walk out on us. May he keep us centered and devoted to him, following the life path he has cleared, watching the signposts, walking at the pace and rhythms he laid down for our ancestors."

1 KINGS 8:56–58 MSG

My beloved and blessed God, there is no promise You have spoken that You have not also fulfilled. Everything You told Moses would happen happened. You and Your words give me rest from all sides, all quarters, all factions within and without. They are my life and breath. Not only are Your words truth, but they also have the power to calm me, to settle me down and make me content. So continue to be with me, Lord. Don't give up on me but keep me with You, centered, a follower of Your way. Amen.

Day 44

STRENGTHENED WITH TRUST

The village. . .had been burned to the ground,
and their wives, sons, and daughters all taken prisoner.
David and his men burst out in loud wails—wept and
wept until they were exhausted with weeping. . . .
There was talk among the men, bitter over the loss
of their families, of stoning him. David strengthened
himself with trust in his God. . . . Then David prayed
to God. . . . David recovered the whole lot.
1 SAMUEL 30:3–4, 6, 8, 19 MSG

Your Word makes clear, Lord, that there are times when it's okay to have a good cry. I should take time to mourn over the losses I suffer in this world. After all, Jesus cried, so why not me? Yet when I'm all cried out, I need to seek Your face so I can find my way out of any why-me conundrums. I garner strength and encouragement by sitting in Your presence. Then I am to pray, asking You what I should do to find a path to restoration. Only when I have received Your instruction am I to take the next steps. For only with Your power can I live out Your plan and be restored to joy once more. Amen.

ALL THE ANSWERS

Humble yourselves before the Lord,
and he will exalt you.
JAMES 4:10 ESV

. . . .

God, I want control. I want to know how life will unfold. I want to have answers for all my questions. How long do I have to wait? What is Your plan? Why am I sitting in the quiet? Where is Your Spirit beckoning?

Do You hear all my questions and the anxiety underneath? Forgive me, God, for worrying—for clinging to answers more than Your presence. Draw me to curl up with You now. To simply be with You and enjoy Your presence, not for the answers I get, but for the intimacy that comes from sitting with You. Where I'm anxious for answers, please whisper that You are the answer—that You know my needs and will take care of me.

I surrender my control. I surrender my angst. I surrender my worry and frantic anxiety. I surrender my need to rush to the next answer before waiting for You to respond. I surrender my security in needing to have a plan. I surrender to You. Amen.

Day 46

THE CHANGE-UP

*The Lord has chosen me to bring good news to poor
people. . .to heal those with a sad heart. . .to tell those
who are being held and those in prison that they can
go free. . . . He has sent me to comfort all who are filled
with sorrow. . . . I will give them a crown of beauty
instead of ashes. . .the oil of joy instead of sorrow,
and a spirit of praise instead of a spirit of no hope.*
ISAIAH 61:1–3 NLV

. . . .

You, Lord, are constantly changing things up in my life.
First You brought me the good news of Your Son, making
me feel richly blessed. Then You made Your way into my
heart. And every time I plant myself in Your Word, I find
You continuing to turn me around. You bring me comfort
when I'm down. You lift my soul from the trappings of
this world so that I can be free once more. Out of a pile
of ashes, You find me roses. When I feel hopeless, You plant
a spirit of praise within me. Continue to change me, Lord,
to let You turn my life around. Amen.

Day 47

NEVERTHELESS

The king and his men went to Jerusalem against the Jebusites, the inhabitants of the land, who said to David, "You will not come in here, but the blind and the lame will ward you off"—thinking, "David cannot come in here." Nevertheless, David took the stronghold of Zion, that is, the city of David. . . . And David became greater and greater, for the LORD, the God of hosts, was with him.
2 SAMUEL 5:6–7, 10 ESV

. . . .

Every success David had, Lord, was because You were with him—*and* David was with You. That's how I want to live my life, Lord. When You call me to do something, when You want me to follow in Jesus' steps and to live out what You have planned for me, I do not want to be dissuaded or discouraged by what other people say. I want to *nevertheless* take the strongholds You want me to take. Win the battles You want me to win. For then, not only will I have the joy of that success, but You will take joy in me as well. Give me that courage, Lord. Be with me in all You would have me do. Help me to live a "nevertheless" life for Your glory. Amen.

Day 48

THE PATH OF PEACE

*You, my child, "Prophet of the Highest," will go ahead
of the Master to prepare his ways, present the offer of
salvation to his people, the forgiveness of their sins.
Through the heartfelt mercies of our God, God's Sunrise
will break in upon us, shining on those in the darkness,
those sitting in the shadow of death, then showing us
the way, one foot at a time, down the path of peace.*
LUKE 1:76–79 MSG

. . . .

You, Lord, are the sunrise of my life. Because of Your mercy
and love, Your light can and does shine on me. You take
me by the hand and lead me out of the darkness of confusion. You muffle the world's noise and begin singing a
love song to me alone. You bring me into the light of Your
being where I am forgiven but not ever forgotten. Thank
You, Lord, for these blessings. Thank You for the way You
patiently nurture and encourage me, whispering Your promise to never ever let me go. And most of all, Lord, thank
You for leading me down the path of Your peace, one slow
step at a time. Amen.

Day 49

EVER-PRESENT SPIRIT

*And he said to them, "Pay attention to what you
hear: with the measure you use, it will be measured
to you, and still more will be added to you."*
MARK 4:24 ESV

. . . .

God, sometimes I forget to notice that You are always with
me. When I am sad, You are with me. Joyful? You are with
me. You tell me that if I go to the heavens, You are there.
And to the depths of the earth, You are still with me. I love
that You are a constant companion, a friend as well as my
Savior.

God, please forgive me for neglecting this truth. For
mistaking Your intimacy for a feeling. You are with me
even when I can't feel You. Even when I'm walking through
the valley, Your Spirit is ever present. I'm quieting myself
now to listen. Help me notice the movement of Your Spirit
in this moment. In this day. In my comings and goings
and thoughts and questions. Awaken me to how personal
and near and constant Your Spirit is in and through me.

I'm so grateful that You are a God I don't have to go to.
You draw near and stay with me. Through every moment.
Amen.

Day 50

BOOMERANG

Go your way; behold, I send you out like lambs into
the midst of wolves. . . . Whatever house you enter,
first say, Peace be to this household! [Freedom from
all the distresses that result from sin be with this family].
And if anyone [worthy] of peace and blessedness is
there, the peace and blessedness you wish shall come
upon him; but if not, it shall come back to you.
LUKE 10:3, 5–6 AMPC

What a wonderful way to spread Your peace, Lord, by taking it on the road. You have a direction for me to take. A path to follow. My job and joy are to trust and follow Your leading. So show me, Lord, where You would have me go, which household You would have me reach out to. Then give me courage to enter into the unknown there and to bless that household with Your peace. . . . Yet if Your peace and blessing are neither wanted nor warranted by that household, I thank You for setting things up so that the peace and blessedness I wish upon others will come back upon me. That's a boomerang result I'll never dodge. Amen!

SAVING POWER

"The Lord says to you, 'Do not be afraid or troubled because of these many men. For the battle is not yours but God's. Go down to fight them tomorrow. . . . You will not need to fight in this battle. Just stand still in your places and see the saving power of the Lord work for you, O Judah and Jerusalem.' Do not be afraid or troubled. Go out against them tomorrow, for the Lord is with you."

2 CHRONICLES 20:15–17 NLV

. . . .

Lord, when forces come up against me, I so often try to fight them on my own, in my own strength, and according to my own game plan. Yet Your Word makes it clear that the very first thing I should do when I'm in trouble is come to You, praising You and thanking You for all the ways You provide for me and work in my life. Then I am to ask what I should do—if I should stand still and watch You fight for me or move out and face my foe with Your strength and courage running through me, knowing that in the end, whatever the result, I *will* rejoice in following Your saving power. Amen.

Day 52

NEW DAY

I saw Holy Jerusalem, new-created, descending
resplendent out of Heaven. . . . I heard a voice thunder
from the Throne: "Look! Look! God has moved into the
neighborhood, making his home with men and women!
They're his people, he's their God. He'll wipe every tear
from their eyes. Death is gone for good—tears gone, crying
gone, pain gone—all the first order of things gone."
The Enthroned continued, "Look! I'm making everything new.
Write it all down—each word dependable and accurate."
REVELATION 21:2–5 MSG

Oh Lord, how I long for the day when the New Jerusalem
will be my home. When You will have moved into my
neighborhood, making Your home among all those who
have been faithful to You. For then there will no longer
be pain and no need for tears. You will be making everything new—even better than the garden of Eden. This is
the hope I cling to, the thought that gives me so much joy
in this world. For each day is a day to make things new,
to let go of my troubles and melt into You. Thank You,
Lord, for gifting me this present day that bears the hope
of tomorrow with You. In Jesus' name, amen.

Day 53

THE POWER OF PRAISE

*"Trust in the Lord your God, and you will be
made strong. Trust in the men who speak for Him,
and you will do well." . . . [Jehoshaphat] called those
who sang to the Lord and those who praised Him
in holy clothing. They went out in front of the army
and said, "Give thanks to the Lord. For His loving-
kindness lasts forever." When they began to sing
and praise, the Lord set traps against the men.*
2 CHRONICLES 20:20–22 NLV

. . . .

It's one thing to read about trusting in You, Lord. It's quite
another thing to actually *do* the trusting. That's where
I sometimes fall short of how and who You want me to be.
Help me work on that, Father. Help me to grow stronger
and stronger by trusting You. Help me to be the brave
woman You created me to be, one who goes out to meet
her enemies while she's singing praises to You. It sounds
crazy, but I'm trusting You to make this work and to bring
me victory in the process, just as You did for Jehoshaphat
and his people who, in the end, "returned to Jerusalem
with joy. For the Lord had filled them with joy by saving
them" (verse 27). Amen.

Day 54

OPEN DOORS

By entering through faith into what God has always
wanted to do for us—set us right with him, make us
fit for him—we have it all together with God because
of our Master Jesus. . . . We throw open our doors
to God and discover at the same moment that he
has already thrown open his door to us. We find
ourselves standing where we always hoped we might
stand—out in the wide open spaces of God's grace
and glory, standing tall and shouting our praise.
ROMANS 5:1–2 MSG

Because of my faith in You, Jesus, I am just where our Father God wants me—right with Him. I now have not just peace with God but access to Him! I've thrown open my door to my Creator only to discover that at that exact same moment, He's thrown His door open to me! There is now nothing between us! No barrier to keep me from my all-powerful provider, my beloved Lord, and one and only Master, Yahweh! In this, I rejoice! In Jesus' name, amen.

LIGHT IN THE DARKNESS

*Again Jesus spoke to them, saying, "I am the light
of the world. Whoever follows me will not walk
in darkness, but will have the light of life."*
JOHN 8:12 ESV

. . . .

Anything that shimmers or hints of light is from You, Lord.
Help me pay attention to this in my innermost being. Where
is there peace? That's of You. Where is there joy? That's
of You. Where is there a sense of feeling alive and whole?
All of this beauty is from You.

I confess that I struggle to celebrate the light until it's
dark. So I'm calling out my gratitude in the light and in
the dark, for You are in all of it.

Where there is anxiety or lack of peace, help me turn
toward Your light. Where there is shame or self-loathing,
help me leave this behind. Where there is doubt and worry,
let me lay this at Your feet. I only want to follow where
You call my name and to believe this path is drenched in
star-laden light. Amen.

Day 56

EVEN THEN

*The Lord is my Light and my Salvation—whom shall
I fear or dread? The Lord is the Refuge and Stronghold
of my life—of whom shall I be afraid? . . . Though a host
encamp against me, my heart shall not fear; though
war arise against me, [even then] in this will I be
confident. One thing have I asked of the Lord, that will
I seek, inquire for, and [insistently] require: that I may
dwell. . .[in His presence] all the days of my life.*

PSALM 27:1, 3–4 AMPC

. . . .

You, Lord, are the one who divided the Red Sea, stopped
the sun, and sent chariots of fire to protect Your prophet.
Throughout the ages, You've continually proven Yourself to
be the God of all gods! So, with You on my side, I need have
no fear. In fact, I am calm. For there's no one who can outdo
You, God Almighty. Even if I'm caught in a war, *even then*
I'll be at peace within because You're here to help me, to
pull me into Your safety net. Continue to be with me, Lord,
loving me, holding me, calming me all the days of my life,
to the end. Even then. Amen.

Day 57

HAPPY FOR HOPE

*Now that we have been made right with God by
putting our trust in Him, we have peace with Him.
It is because of what our Lord Jesus Christ did for
us. By putting our trust in God, He has given us His
loving-favor and has received us. We are happy for
the hope we have of sharing the shining-greatness
of God. We are glad for our troubles also.
We know that troubles help us learn not to give up.*
ROMANS 5:1–3 NLV

. . . .

Oh Lord Jesus, thank You for loving me so much that You
died to save my soul. You sacrificed to make me right with
God so that I can have access to Him through prayer and
praises. This gives me such peace. It's clear I cannot make
it through this life without You by my side, without looking
to You for an example of what I am to do and say. Now,
as I trust God with all my heart, mind, soul, and strength,
I can have joy no matter my situation. No matter what
troubles come against me, I will never give up for I have
hope, knowing You will help me through thick and thin,
life and death. Amen.

Day 58

EVEN STRONGER

Pure gold put in the fire comes out of it proved pure;
genuine faith put through this suffering comes out proved
genuine. When Jesus wraps this all up, it's your faith,
not your gold, that God will have on display as evidence
of his victory. You never saw him, yet you love him.
You still don't see him, yet you trust him—with laughter
and singing. Because you kept on believing, you'll get
what you're looking forward to: total salvation.

1 PETER 1:7–9 MSG

Even when I'm having trouble in my life, Jesus, there's one thing that keeps me going: You. Knowing You are with me. Knowing You walked a much harder road than I am now on and managed, with every test, to come out stronger on the other side. Jesus, although I have never actually seen You, I know You are here. You are the one I can trust. Your promises are what I can hope in. With You by my side and Your Word written in my heart and echoing in my mind, I can face anything with joy and laughter. In Your name, amen!

Day 59

GOD'S BLESSINGS

*You shall keep the Feast of Weeks to the Lord your
God with a tribute of a freewill offering from your
hand, which you shall give to the Lord your God,
as the Lord your God blesses you. . . . You shall rejoice
in your Feast. . .because the Lord your God will
bless you in all your produce and in all the works of
your hands, so that you will be altogether joyful.*
DEUTERONOMY 16:10, 14–15 AMPC

. . . .

I can't remember the last time I came to You with nothing
but praise and thanks, Lord, for all the ways You've blessed
me. Instead, I seem to mostly either unload my troubles or
ask You for things. So today, Lord, I come to You wanting
nothing, only giving You thanks. Thank You for saving me,
loving me, protecting me, and watching over me. Thank
You for the food, clothing, and shelter You so adequately
provide. Thank You for blessings seen and unseen. And
thank You for blessing the work I put my hands to, so that
I can be "altogether joyful." What a great God You are! All
praise and glory to You, dear Lord. Amen.

Day 60

IN THE LAND OF THE LIVING

*Your face (Your presence), Lord, will I seek,
inquire for, and require. . . . [What, what would have
become of me] had I not believed that I would see the
Lord's goodness in the land of the living! Wait and
hope for and expect the Lord; be brave and of good
courage and let your heart be stout and enduring.
Yes, wait for and hope for and expect the Lord.*
PSALM 27:8, 13–14 AMPC

. . . .

I seek You and Your face, Lord. I search for Your wisdom.
I require Your presence. For You alone get me through
the hard days. You alone give me the peace I need amid
the battle. You alone give me the courage to face another
hour, day, week, month. When things get very difficult, Your
Word gives me the hope I need to carry on. I don't know
what would have become of me if I had not anticipated,
expected, and watched for Your goodness in the land of
the living. For You, Lord, I wait with courage and hope
with great expectation. In Jesus' name, amen.

Day 61

A WELL-STEWARDED GIFT

*Do everything readily and cheerfully—no bickering,
no second-guessing allowed! Go out into the world
uncorrupted, a breath of fresh air in this squalid
and polluted society. Provide people with a glimpse
of good living and of the living God. Carry the light-
giving Message into the night so I'll have good cause
to be proud of you on the day that Christ returns.*
PHILIPPIANS 2:14–16 MSG

. . . .

You know what's funny, Lord? The very quality I was criti-
cizing in someone is his greatest gift! I was focusing on his
boundless energy and intense joy, but to have energy and
use that passion to turn outward is a well-stewarded gift.

Lord, please forgive my criticalness. I admit, I'd rather
have energy than sit idly and only move toward selfish
desires. I want to use every ounce of energy I have to be
a mirror of Your love and grace.

I ask You for the energy and stamina and soul joy to
run passionately toward a selfless life—a life where I aim
to serve, not be served. A life where I love before I'm loved.
A life where I acknowledge that You are in all people and
they are worthy to be respected and known. Thank You,
Lord. Amen.

Day 62

CUDDLED AND CODDLED

"You have been helped by Me before you were born and carried since you were born. Even when you are old I will be the same. And even when your hair turns white, I will help you. I will take care of what I have made. I will carry you, and will save you. . . . I am God, and there is no other. I am God, and there is no one like Me."

ISAIAH 46:3–4, 9 NLV

. . . .

It's hard to imagine, Lord, that You helped me *before I was even born*—and that *since* then, You continued to carry me, looking out for me, watching over me, and helping me. That in itself gives me a great sense of peace. But further, You tell me that even when I'm old and gray, You'll still be there. You'll still carry me and rescue me. Ah, what sweet calm flows over me. How wonderful to know I'm still a babe in Your arms. I'm still someone who is and desires to be cuddled and coddled. It's true: there is no one like You, Daddy God. For that I am ever grateful! Amen.

Day 63

SINGING AND DANCING

David went everywhere that Saul sent him, and did well. Saul had him lead the men of war. And it was pleasing to all the people and to Saul's servants. When David returned from killing the Philistine, the women came out of all the cities of Israel, singing and dancing, to meet King Saul, playing songs of joy on timbrels. The women sang as they played, and said, "Saul has killed his thousands, and David his ten thousands."

1 SAMUEL 18:5–7 NLV

. . . .

It's so easy to cheer for and celebrate people who play sports or act on stage and screen. But when it comes to celebrating You, Lord, I seem to hesitate, wondering what people will think of me. Help me to change that up, dear God. I want to be like the women who sang and danced with abandon back in David's day. For doing so not only pleases You but fills me with such joy, lifting me higher in mind, spirit, and body. It's a win-win for both of us, Lord. So I come to You with abandon today, dancing as I sing my song of praise, just for You! Amen.

Day 64

STANDING WORD

"I tell from the beginning what will happen in the end. And from times long ago I tell of things which have not been done, saying, 'My Word will stand. And I will do all that pleases Me.' I call a strong and hungry bird from the east, the man from a far country who will do what I have planned. I have spoken, and I will make it happen. I have planned it, and I will do it."
ISAIAH 46:10–11 NLV

. . . .

Lord, it's amazing how well Your Bible books fit together. How the Old Testament supports the New. How the Psalms soothe minds, bodies, souls, and spirits unlike any other book. How the Gospels tell Your story with four different audiences in mind. How the letters to the New Testament churches tell us how to live, and how Jesus' Revelation tells us what to expect when He returns. Lord, Your Word not only stands but transforms people as well as circumstances. What You have said, You *will* make happen. What You have planned, You *will* do. Help me to rest in the peace of that promise, Lord. Speak to me. Tell me what part You would have me play in Your plan. In Jesus' name, amen.

Day 65

TURNED HEARTS

They finished their building by decree of the
God of Israel and by decree of Cyrus and Darius
and Artaxerxes king of Persia. . . . And the
people of Israel. . .celebrated the dedication of
this house of God with joy. . . . For the LORD had
made them joyful and had turned the heart of
the king of Assyria to them, so that he aided
them in the work of the house of God.

EZRA 6:14, 16, 22 ESV

Only You, Lord, have the power to turn the hearts of rulers,
whether they be queens, presidents, tyrants, or dictators,
so that Your work can be accomplished through them and
us. This gives me hope that You can turn even the most
godless person to help Your people do what You have called
them to do, no matter how great the task. And that hope
in You and Your power working to change people, against
all odds and appearances to the contrary, gives me great
joy. For with You, nothing is impossible. In Your power I
not only rest, but go forward with confidence, hope, and
joy. In Jesus' name, amen.

Day 66

RAIN

"Yet he has not left himself without testimony:
He has shown kindness by giving you rain from
heaven and crops in their seasons; he provides you
with plenty of food and fills your hearts with joy."
ACTS 14:17 NIV

It's drizzly and cold and raining outside. As I watch the drops fall, I think of how often You are watering and tending to the garden of our lives. God, where are the seeds You have planted? Where are the seeds I have planted? What does the ground look like?

Even as You rain, You are watering what needs to sprout from the soil. I'm thankful for rain today—how it washes and clears and goes deep to the seeds that need to sprout. Rain is like forgiveness. Rain washes away all the extra and gets me to the heart of the matter.

What is in my heart? What is it blooming? Is it blooming beauty? Weeds? May this blooming be a clear indication of what I'm planting and how Your watering is bringing things to life. May my life be a garden of beauty and forgiveness. Amen.

Day 67

TEACHINGS

I am happy to find some of your children living in the truth as the Father has said we should. . . . Anyone who goes too far and does not live by the teachings of Christ does not have God. If you live by what Christ taught, you have both the Father and the Son. . . . I hope to come to you soon. Then we can talk about these things together that your joy may be full.

2 JOHN 1:4, 9, 12 NLV

. . . .

Lord, I want to please You beyond any church doctrine or tradition. I want to follow You and Your teachings—not my own idea of what is right and wrong. To walk just as Your Word outlines for me. Yet I don't want to run ahead of what You would have me be, say, or do. So, Lord Jesus, reveal to me what You would have me know. Teach me the right way to live. For when I understand Your way, I know I'll be walking God's way. And that's the only right way. On Your path is where all my joy, strength, hope, and rest lie. Guide me, Lord. Teach me Your wisdom. Show me Your path from here to eternity. Amen.

Day 68

MORNING MOMENTS

In the morning You hear my voice, O Lord; in the morning I prepare [a prayer, a sacrifice] for You and watch and wait [for You to speak to my heart]. . . . Let all those who take refuge and put their trust in You rejoice; let them ever sing and shout for joy, because You make a covering over them and defend them; let those also who love Your name be joyful in You and be in high spirits.
PSALM 5:3, 11 AMPC

In these early morning moments, Lord, I come to You. Hear my voice. I'm giving You my all—my heart, soul, body, and mind. I await Your presence. Come to me, Lord. Speak gently, softly, to my heart. Tell me the words You want me to hear as I take refuge in You, laying down all my burdens and taking up Your strength, courage, and love. Fill me with Your Spirit. Shield me from any dangers that may come. Help me stay attuned to You all through this day. Lord, I love You ever so much, to the moon and back and more. For it is with and in You that I find my true joy every moment of the day. Amen.

Day 69

FOREVER THE SAME

The heavens are the work of Your hands. They shall perish, but You shall remain and endure; yes, all of them shall wear out and become old like a garment. Like clothing You shall change them, and they shall be changed and pass away. But You remain the same, and Your years shall have no end. . . . Jesus Christ (the Messiah) is [always] the same, yesterday, today, [yes] and forever (to the ages).
PSALM 102:25–27; HEBREWS 13:8 AMPC

. . . .

Your creation surrounds me, Lord. Your mountains, skies, creeks, grass, earth, birds, wind, rain, snow, sun, stones, stars, bunnies, and deer are continually changing, shifting, transforming. Someday they may fall aside, fade out, blow away, and be gone forever. It's quite unsettling, being caught in a world of continual change. Yet then I think of You and realize that although creation may change, You, the Creator, never will. You are a forever God. Through Jesus You have opened the gateway to eternity, have made a way for me to live with You. So today I rest in the peace of the unchangeable You, both now and forever. Amen.

Day 70

HEALING POWER

A gentle tongue [with its healing power] is a tree of life. . . . A man has joy in making an apt answer, and a word spoken at the right moment—how good it is! . . . The mind of the [uncompromisingly] righteous studies how to answer. . . . The light in the eyes [of him whose heart is joyful] rejoices the hearts of others, and good news nourishes the bones.

PROVERBS 15:4, 23, 28, 30 AMPC

. . . .

Lord, please reign over and rein in my tongue. There are so many times I speak without thinking and end up hurting others. I want to follow the steps of Christ, Lord—to build people up, not tear them down. So help me, Lord, to have a gentle tongue that heals others so they can grow closer to You. I want to increase the joys of others with a balm, not destroy them with a bomb. Help me to study how to answer before I speak and to think before I let one word cross my lips. For then not only I, but those with whom I speak, will be filled with joy. Amen.

Day 71

GETTING A GRIP

*There's one other thing I remember, and remembering,
I keep a grip on hope: God's loyal love couldn't have run
out, his merciful love couldn't have dried up. They're
created new every morning. How great your faithfulness!
I'm sticking with God (I say it over and over). He's all
I've got left. God proves to be good to the man who
passionately waits, to the woman who diligently seeks.*

Lamentations 3:21–25 MSG

. . . .

Some days, Lord, it seems relatively easy to lose hope. The
problems to be tackled seem to be growing by the minute.
It's enough to make even the strongest of believers despair!
But I'm leaning into You, Lord. I'm remembering how every
morning with You is a new beginning. Because You have
unlimited mercy and love, You create them new every
morning! That's how faithful You are to me even when
I might hesitate to be faithful to You! Forgive me, Lord, for
my missteps. For You are my all in all, my greatest hope,
my everlasting love. I will continue to seek You and adore
You always, for in You I find my peace. Amen.

Day 72

THE FRIEND WHO
DOESN'T KNOW CHRIST

*For by grace you have been saved through faith.
And this is not your own doing; it is the gift of God, not a
result of works, so that no one may boast. For we are his
workmanship, created in Christ Jesus for good works, which
God prepared beforehand, that we should walk in them.*

EPHESIANS 2:8–10 ESV

. . . .

Jesus, I have a dear friend who doesn't know You. Help me not look at our time together as rushed or to be used to get her to arrive at Your doorstep. Instead, let us just be friends. Let us learn from one another. Help me trust that all truth is Your truth and that by being myself, Your Spirit is working and alive.

I draw on Your Spirit now. Forgive me for believing for a hot second that any of her salvation depends on our friendship. Please remove this holier-than-thou mindset and replace it with the joy of journeying with her and inviting her to pay attention to Your work.

And one day when she comes to know You, may I be there to celebrate and remember all the ways You invited and stirred her to Your Spirit. Thank You for the mysterious ways in which You work. Amen.

Day 73

THE LIGHT

The teachers and those who are wise shall shine like the brightness of the firmament, and those who turn many to righteousness (to uprightness and right standing with God) [shall give forth light] like the stars forever and ever. . . . The light of the [uncompromisingly] righteous [is within him—it grows brighter and] rejoices, but the lamp of the wicked [furnishes only a derived, temporary light and] shall be put out shortly.
DANIEL 12:3; PROVERBS 13:9 AMPC

. . . .

I want to shine for You, Lord. To walk right in step with You and to keep on Your pathway. Abba God, Your Son said, "I am the Light of the world. He who follows Me will not be walking in the dark, but will have the Light which is Life" (John 8:12 AMPC). Thank You for allowing Jesus' light in this dark world to reveal more of You. In this moment, Lord, show me Your bright presence. Shine Your light—which overcomes all darkness and banishes the sorrow that comes with it—into me right now. Make me glow for You and then reflect Your light onto others, spreading Your joy and shining forevermore. In Jesus' name, amen.

Day 74

A GLAD HEART

A glad heart makes a cheerful countenance, but by sorrow of heart the spirit is broken. . . . All the days of the desponding and afflicted are made evil [by anxious thoughts and forebodings], but he who has a glad heart has a continual feast [regardless of circumstances]. Better is little with the reverent, worshipful fear of the Lord than great and rich treasure and trouble with it.
PROVERBS 15:13, 15–16 AMPC

. . . .

Abba, some days I find myself brought so low by what's happening in the world. And sometimes my chin is on the floor because of what's happening in my home, my family, or my work. More often than not, my mind is filled with anxious thoughts and forebodings. But I don't want to live that way. I want to have a glad heart—no matter what's happening. So I need Your help to focus on the good things, the things above, not the things of this earth. Help me, Lord, not to worry about anything— money, relationships, wars, or other troubles—but to keep my chin up by keeping my eyes and focus on You alone. In Jesus' name, amen.

Day 75

WELL-VERSED

Your Word have I hid in my heart, that I may not sin against You. Great and honored are You, O Lord. Teach me Your Law. I have told with my lips of all the Laws of Your mouth. I have found as much joy in following Your Law as one finds in much riches. I will think about Your Law and have respect for Your ways. I will be glad in Your Law. I will not forget Your Word.

PSALM 119:11–16 NLV

. . . .

Your Word, Lord, is such a treasure. There is nothing I value more, nothing that gives me more hope and joy than hearing and understanding You and Your Word. Teach me what I need to learn today. Help me hide all my knowledge of You within my most sacred place. Then in times of trouble or challenge, I'll have a reserve of Your wisdom that I can pull from to regain my confidence, courage, and joy. Mark out the reading path You would have me take. Show me the words You would have me write upon my heart so that I will be well versed when I need their power. In Jesus' name, amen.

IN THE ARMS OF THE BELOVED SHEPHERD

Like an apple tree among the trees of the wood, so is my beloved [shepherd] among the sons [cried the girl]! Under his shadow I delighted to sit, and his fruit was sweet to my taste. . . . His banner over me was love [for love waved as a protecting and comforting banner over my head when I was near him]. . . . [I can feel] his left hand under my head and his right hand embraces me!
SONG OF SOLOMON 2:3–4, 6 AMPC

. . . .

Beloved Shepherd, I find more delight, more joy in Your presence than anywhere else. For You have told me of Your deep love, which will never die but continue to protect and comfort me whenever You are near. So I come to You in this tender and precious moment. I can feel Your left hand under my head and Your right hand pulling me close into Your loving embrace. As my head rests against Your breast, I rise and fall with each of Your breaths. Hold me close, Lord. Keep me safe as I linger here in Your presence, safe in body, sound in mind, and happy in heart. Amen.

Day 77

ENTER THE SILENCE

It's a good thing to quietly hope, quietly hope for help from GOD. It's a good thing when you're young to stick it out through the hard times. When life is heavy and hard to take, go off by yourself. Enter the silence. Bow in prayer. Don't ask questions: Wait for hope to appear. Don't run from trouble. Take it full-face. The "worst" is never the worst.
LAMENTATIONS 3:26–30 MSG

. . . .

It's been a long few days, Lord. And I need some time away with You. Some time to sit quietly and tap into Your power and grace, to reacquaint myself with Your Word and the hope I find there. I need to step back, step away from the daily grind, even if only for a moment. Perhaps only for this very moment. Right here, right now, Lord, I come to You. I enter the silence, and I bow in prayer. Here I await Your blessing of hope, confidence, courage, and trust. In Jesus' name I wait and pray, amen.

Day 78

I AM ALIVE!

"Look, I am coming soon! My reward is with me, and I will give to each person according to what they have done. I am the Alpha and the Omega, the First and the Last, the Beginning and the End."
REVELATION 22:12–13 NIV

Lord, this journey toward forgiveness is possible only because I am alive in You. You breathe life into my soul. You offer hope for the day ahead. You stir me toward repentance and confession and thankfulness. Time after time. Day after day. Every day is an invitation to live alive. To believe in Your love and let it root down to my bones and blossom high and beautiful so that others can partake in Your shade and beauty.

Today is another chance to forgive—to look inward and to surrender the parts that weigh me down in exchange for Your easy yoke. Thank You for journeying with me as I learn and relearn how to live alive and how to forgive myself and others.

Though I'll never forgive as fully as You did on the cross, God, I am grateful to live alive—free of resentment, washed in Your blood, and basking in Your grace. Amen.

Day 79

SPIRITUAL MOTHERS

*I remember you night and day in my prayers,
and when, as I recall your tears, I yearn to see you so
that I may be filled with joy. I am calling up memories
of your sincere and unqualified faith (the leaning of your
entire personality on God in Christ in absolute trust
and confidence in His power, wisdom, and goodness),
[a faith] that first lived permanently in [the heart of]
your grandmother Lois and your mother Eunice and
now, I am [fully] persuaded, [dwells] in you also.*
2 TIMOTHY 1:3–5 AMPC

. . . .

When I think back on all the women in my life who've
helped me find my way to You, Lord, I cannot help but
wonder how You've worked through them. Because of
these spiritual mothers and grandmothers, I have a faith
that brings me such joy and comfort. For they started me
on the right road, helping me find a way to trust You and
have confidence in You, Your power, and Your wisdom.
Now help me, Lord, to pay forward the joys and blessings
of knowing You. Help me become a spiritual mother to
others. Show me whom I can help train up or support.
Then give me the wisdom and courage to speak to her,
heart-to-heart. Amen.

RISING UP TO THE LOVE

Arise, my love, my fair one, and come away. [So I went with him, and when we were climbing the rocky steps up the hillside, my beloved shepherd said to me] O my dove, [while you are here]. . .in the sheltered and secret place of the cliff, let me see your face, let me hear your voice; for your voice is sweet, and your face is lovely. [My heart was touched and I fervently sang to him my desire].
SONG OF SOLOMON 2:13–15 AMPC

It fills me with joy, Lord, that You call me "my love." That You want me to come away with You to that secret place where we meet, just You and me alone. That You want to see my face and hear my voice. That You think I'm lovely. Thank You, my beloved, for calling me to rise up to You and tell You about my desires and all the things that are on my heart. There is nothing and no one like You, Lord. To You alone I bear all my secrets, all my longings, knowing that You will not laugh at them but will treasure them. Dear heart, I love You. Amen.

Day 81

AN ABUNDANCE OF PEACE

For yet a little while, and the evildoers will be no more; though you look with care where they used to be, they will not be found. But the meek [in the end] shall inherit the earth and shall delight themselves in the abundance of peace. . . . Better is the little that the [uncompromisingly] righteous have than the abundance [of possessions] of many who are wrong and wicked.

Psalm 37:10–11, 16 AMPC

It's good to know, Lord, that the good guys will eventually win out over the bad ones. That at some point, those who have carried out evil plans, those who've harmed themselves or others, will one day have their comeuppance. That someday the meek will end up inheriting the earth and delighting in a wealth of peace on earth. In the meantime, Lord, help me keep my eyes on You, live a "right" life, and leave all the judgment of others to You. Help me obey You at every crossroad, turn where You'd have me turn, do what You'd have me do. To be as my Jesus, meek and gentle, yet firm and strong. In His name, I pray. Amen.

A HEART AWAKE

I went to sleep, but my heart stayed awake. [I dreamed that I heard] the voice of my beloved as he knocked [at the door of my mother's cottage]. Open to me, my sister, my love, my dove, my spotless one [he said]. . . . [But weary from a day in the vineyards, I had already sought my rest] I had put off my garment—how could I [again] put it on? I had washed my feet—how could I [again] soil them?

SONG OF SOLOMON 5:2–3 AMPC

. . . .

Lord, in Your presence I experience such unfathomable joy. Yet at times I am so worn out from earthly cares that I do not open my door to You. In those moments I miss out on Your peace, calm, wisdom, power, strength, and gentle touch. Even in the night hours, asleep or awake, I want to be available to You—to Your voice, Your whisper, Your knock upon my door. Help me keep attuned to Your quest for me. May my spirit be so linked to Yours that I don't know where I stop and You begin. I pray this in Jesus' precious name, amen.

Day 83

BLAST FROM THE PAST

*One thing I do: Forgetting what is behind and reaching
forward to what is ahead, I pursue as my goal the
prize promised by God's heavenly call in Christ Jesus.
Therefore, all who are mature should think this way.
And if you think differently about anything, God
will reveal this also to you. In any case, we should
live up to whatever truth we have attained.*
PHILIPPIANS 3:13–16 HCSB

Too often, Lord, my past encroaches upon then disrupts
my present. The mistakes I had once made, the consequences that followed, keep reverberating in my head.
That sometimes makes it difficult for me to keep my focus
on You, the present, and what You'd have me do in the
moments that make up a day. So help me, Lord, to find
my peace by forgetting what has happened before, what
cannot be undone, and then help me reach forward to
what lies ahead of me as I follow after You. Show me,
Lord. Reveal Yourself and Your plan to me. Point out to
me the way You'd have me go as I blast away from the
past. Amen.

Day 84

JOYFULLY RADIANT

*[She proudly said] I am my beloved's, and his desire
is toward me! . . . Many waters cannot quench love,
neither can floods drown it. . . . [Joyfully the radiant
bride turned to him, the one altogether lovely,
the chief among ten thousand to her soul, and with
unconcealed eagerness to begin her life of sweet
companionship with him, she answered] Make haste,
my beloved, and come quickly, like a gazelle or a
young hart [and take me to our waiting home].*
SONG OF SOLOMON 7:10; 8:7, 14 AMPC

. . . .

The fact that You desire me, Lord, fills me with such delight.
I rejoice that I am Yours and You are mine and that the
love we have for each other can never disappear. I am so
eager to turn to You, to begin our life together each morning. Take me to that rock that is higher than I, that secret
place where it is only You and me, together forever. That
is my true home, my true abode, where nothing untoward
can touch me and where You cover me with Your love. You
dry my tears and simply hold me, telling me all is and will
be well. You are my heaven on earth. Amen.

Day 85

BENEATH THE WINGS

He who dwells in the secret place of the Most High shall remain stable and fixed under the shadow of the Almighty [Whose power no foe can withstand]. I will say of the Lord, He is my Refuge and my Fortress, my God; on Him I lean and rely, and in Him I [confidently] trust! . . . He will cover you with His pinions, and under His wings shall you trust and find refuge.

PSALM 91:1–2, 4 AMPC

. . . .

There is a place like no other. It is here that I find You. In the silence, in the smile of a child, the call of a bird, the rustle of a leaf, the smell of rain, I am swept away to another time and place in You. It is here that I can truly breathe. It is in Your presence that I find the warmth, light, and calm I need to repair and recharge. It is in this secret place that I can find my feet, knowing I'm secure beneath the wings of the Almighty. Hold me here, Lord, my refuge and fortress. Give me the love, peace, and strength I need to find and walk Your way today. Amen.

Day 86

BEYOND UNDERSTANDING

*Be full of joy always because you belong to the Lord.
Again I say, be full of joy! Let all people see how
gentle you are. . . . Do not worry. Learn to pray about
everything. Give thanks to God as you ask Him for
what you need. The peace of God is much greater
than the human mind can understand. This peace will
keep your hearts and minds through Christ Jesus.*
PHILIPPIANS 4:4–7 NLV

Joy, at times, seems elusive, Lord. But that's only because I forget to call on You, my champion, my Master, my Creator, the all-powerful one who makes the seemingly impossible possible! Instead of running to You, I let my worries begin a running dialogue in my head. Soon they spin out of control and build up to a sort of mild panic. Help me, Lord, to learn to pray about anything and everything—and to thank You in the process. For Your Word says that if I do, Your peace beyond understanding will surround me and guard me. So here I am, Lord, telling You all, thanking You for all. . . . Ah, now it's time to rejoice! Amen.

Day 87

A JOYFUL CELEBRATION

Relax, everything's going to be all right;
rest, everything's coming together; open your hearts,
love is on the way! . . . Carefully build yourselves
up in this most holy faith by praying in the Holy
Spirit, staying right at the center of God's love,
keeping your arms open and outstretched, ready
for the mercy of our Master, Jesus Christ. This
is the unending life, the real life! . . . And now to
him who can keep you on your feet. . .fresh and
celebrating. . .be glory, majesty, strength, and rule.
JUDE 1:2, 20–21, 24 MSG

. . . .

I want to build my faith in You, Lord, so that I no longer get caught up in the tears, pain, and sorrows of this world and forget about all the hopes I have in You. So give me Your peace, Lord. Remind me all is and will be okay. Give me the rest I need each day. Help me open my heart, praying in the Spirit and residing in Your presence and love. I'm keeping my arms wide open for You, ready to receive and return Your love. Keep me on my feet, Lord, standing strong as You lead me in a joyful celebration of this magnificent life of faith! Amen.

Day 88

HUMBLY BLESSED

*He opened His mouth and taught them, saying: Blessed
(happy, to be envied, and spiritually prosperous—with
life-joy and satisfaction in God's favor and salvation,
regardless of their outward conditions) are the poor in
spirit (the humble, who rate themselves insignificant),
for theirs is the kingdom of heaven! . . . [Jesus] poured
water into the washbasin and began to wash the disciples'
feet and to wipe them with the [servant's] towel.*
MATTHEW 5:2–3; JOHN 13:5 AMPC

. . . .

Jesus, I can't imagine being one of the disciples whose
feet You washed. It seems incomprehensible that You, the
Son of God, would kneel before one of Your brothers or
sisters and wash his or her dirty, stinky feet. Yet that's
just what You did—providing the example I am to follow
as Your disciple. Today help me, Lord, to have a servant's
heart and to humble myself, kneeling before someone who
needs my help, no matter who or what that person is. For
I want to share in Your joy, to be blessed in and with You,
and to gain the kingdom of heaven! In Your name, amen.

Day 89

SUPERNATURAL PROTECTION

*Because you have made the Lord your refuge, and the
Most High your dwelling place, there shall no evil befall
you, nor any plague or calamity come near your tent.
For He will give His angels [especial] charge over you
to accompany and defend and preserve you in all your
ways [of obedience and service]. They shall bear you up
on their hands, lest you dash your foot against a stone.*
PSALM 91:9–12 AMPC

. . . .

The idea of angels watching over me is so precious, Lord.
Yet it's not just an idea—it's a *reality*. Because I have made
You my safe place, You've given Your angels charge over
me. You've sent them to walk with me, take care of me,
and protect me in all I do. They've been instructed to hold
me up in their hands so I don't stumble and fall when
the road gets rough. You as my safe place. . .supernatural
protection. . .a sure refuge—all these things lead to peace
and to You, Lord, my provider of peace. Amen.

Day 90

WORDS OF JOY

O Lord, You know and understand; [earnestly]
remember me and visit me and avenge me on my
persecutors. Take me not away [from joy or from
life itself] in Your long-suffering [to my enemies];
know that for Your sake I suffer and bear reproach.
Your words were found, and I ate them; and Your
words were to me a joy and the rejoicing of my heart,
for I am called by Your name, O Lord God of hosts.
JEREMIAH 15:15–16 AMPC

God, I am so glad You can see what I'm going through, all the things I'm up against. You know how my troubles are zapping my joy. But then I reach for Your Word. I open Your Book and discover You. Letter by letter, word by word, sentence by sentence, I absorb all You have to say to me—how You love and work with me, how You want all that is good to come to me. You even have a plan for me. And it is here, within Your Word and presence, that I find the joy I need to live this life. Thank You for allowing me to hear Your voice and find my way home to You. Amen.

PERSONAL KNOWLEDGE

Because he has set his love upon Me, therefore will I deliver him; I will set him on high, because he knows and understands My name [has a personal knowledge of My mercy, love, and kindness—trusts and relies on Me, knowing I will never forsake him, no, never]. He shall call upon Me, and I will answer him; I will be with him in trouble, I will deliver him.

PSALM 91:14–15 AMPC

. . . .

The more I learn about You, Lord, the more I love You. The more I understand what You have done for me, the more I trust You. There are, of course, some things I may never know, but I'm okay with that because I have confidence in You for not just one or two things but for *all* things. I trust that You have a plan for me. That You will answer my call if ever I'm in trouble. That You will come to me and be with me in the *midst* of trouble. That You will never let me go. Because with You and me, Lord, it's personal. What love, what peace, what protection I have in You! Amen.

Day 92

MIND OVER MATTERS

*Keep your minds thinking about whatever is true,
whatever is respected, whatever is right, whatever
is pure, whatever can be loved, and whatever is
well thought of. If there is anything good and worth
giving thanks for, think about these things. Keep
on doing all the things you learned and received
and heard from me. Do the things you saw me do.
Then the God Who gives peace will be with you.*
PHILIPPIANS 4:8–9 NLV

. . . .

Too often, Lord, I find myself so engrossed in the bad things
happening in the world that I forget about all the good
that surrounds me—You and Your Word included. So help
me lift my thoughts in Your direction, Lord. I want to fill
my mind and meditate on things that are good, true, and
uplifting. I want to think the best, not the worst; of the
lovely, not the unlovely. I want to think of things to praise,
not things to criticize. But I need Your help. Make it my
desire, Lord, to fill my mind with You before I reach for
the paper or turn on the news. For I know that if I'm full
of You and Your goodness, I won't have room for anything
else—but joy. Amen.

GREAT THINGS AWAIT

"Do not be distressed or angry with yourselves because you sold me here, for God sent me before you to preserve life. . . . God sent me before you. . .to keep alive for you many survivors. So it was not you who sent me here, but God. He has made me a father to Pharaoh, and lord of all his house and ruler over all the land of Egypt."

GENESIS 45:5, 7–8 ESV

. . . .

When I'm lying awake at night wondering, *Why me?* or *What did I do to deserve this?* I inevitably come back to Joseph. All the things that he'd been through—sold to slave traders by his brothers, unjustly accused of a crime, thrown into a dungeon, then forgotten and neglected—would be enough to crush such a dreamer, to turn his stomach into a knot of anxiety and frustration. But instead, Joseph stuck with God, stayed calm, and carried on, continually going on to the next thing, knowing that God was in control and that great things awaited him! That's how I want to be, Lord. As calm, cool, and collected as Joseph, during good times and bad. Amen.

Day 94

TENDER TEARS OF LOVE

*He opened His mouth and taught them, saying: . . . Blessed
and enviably happy [with a happiness produced by the
experience of God's favor and especially conditioned by the
revelation of His matchless grace] are those who mourn,
for they shall be comforted! . . . He said, Where have you
laid him? They said to Him, Lord, come and see. Jesus
wept. The Jews said, See how [tenderly] He loved him!*
MATTHEW 5:2, 4; JOHN 11:34–36 AMPC

You, Jesus, are well aware of all the sorrows I have suffered,
for You Yourself are called "a Man of sorrows and pains, and
acquainted with grief" (Isaiah 53:3 AMPC). When You were looking for Your friend Lazarus, knowing he had died, You wept
tears of tender pity and love. Yet You have taught that even
in my sorrows, I can find joy. For You, who know what I've
gone through, will comfort me. And it is that comfort I seek
now. Be with me, Lord. Wipe away my tender tears. Hold
me in Your arms until I once again experience gladness
in You. Amen.

Day 95

NOTHING LOST

Jesus then took the loaves, and when he had given thanks,
he distributed them to those who were seated. So also the
fish, as much as they wanted. And when they had eaten
their fill, he told his disciples, "Gather up the leftover
fragments, that nothing may be lost." So they gathered
them up and filled twelve baskets with fragments from
the five barley loaves left by those who had eaten.
JOHN 6:11–13 ESV

Lord, You are continually amazing me with Your power, wisdom, and creativity, all of which shine through the stories in Your Word. Each day, I reach for Your Book and find a new lesson, a new treasure, a new phrase that draws me closer to knowing You. Today I'm reminded of how well You provide for me, how prayers and faith move me in the telling and doing, and then move You to provide a miracle, to go beyond a point I thought unreachable. Today I find my peace knowing that You, Lord, are the ultimate provider, the God of wonder, the Spirit of light. Thank You for never allowing anything to be lost. Even me. Amen.

Day 96

GLAD IN GOD

I'm glad in God, far happier than you would ever guess. . . . I don't have a sense of needing anything personally. I've learned by now to be quite content whatever my circumstances. I'm just as happy with little as with much, with much as with little. I've found the recipe for being happy whether full or hungry, hands full or hands empty. Whatever I have, wherever I am, I can make it through anything in the One who makes me who I am.

PHILIPPIANS 4:10–13 MSG

So many people are miserable, Lord. They are always in a state of wanting, never quite feeling complete and happy. I must admit that sometimes I find myself there too. I am envious of others and what they have and can do. But then I think of You, and all those desires fade. I find myself quite content, even happy with what I have and what's happening in my life. For You, Lord, are all I need. With You giving me strength, grace, mercy, love, hope, and so much more, I'm happy whether my pantry is full or empty, my house warm or cold, my bank balance overflowing or sparse. I'm at peace and glad in You. Amen.

Day 97

QUEEN OF THE HILL

Though the cherry trees don't blossom and the strawberries don't ripen, though the apples are worm-eaten and the wheat fields stunted, though the sheep pens are sheepless and the cattle barns empty, I'm singing joyful praise to GOD. I'm turning cartwheels of joy to my Savior God. Counting on GOD's Rule to prevail, I take heart and gain strength. I run like a deer. I feel like I'm king of the mountain!
HABAKKUK 3:17–19 MSG

Lord, no matter how things are going in my life, no matter how many troubles or trials assail me, I will continue to trust You. Because that's where my joy lies. My confidence in You is what keeps me going merrily along, singing joyful praises to You and Your name! Even amid loss, I trust You to keep me whole and hearty, pleased and pleasant. I'm gaining my strength in You. You are the one who will give me the power to keep on going, to step out of my comfort zone and into Your plan for my life. Even when others are struck low, I'll be standing sure-footed on Your mountaintop, queen of the hill with the Lord of love. Amen.

Day 98

A QUIET STRENGTH

*Blessed (happy, blithesome, joyous, spiritually
prosperous—with life-joy and satisfaction in God's
favor and salvation, regardless of their outward
conditions) are the meek (the mild, patient, long-
suffering), for they shall inherit the earth! . . .
Say to the Daughter of Zion. . .Behold, your King is
coming to you, lowly and riding on a donkey,
and on a colt, the foal of a donkey [a beast of burden].*
MATTHEW 5:5; 21:5 AMPC

. . . .

When I think about it, it doesn't seem like I'd be very
happy being meek, Jesus. Yet that is what You were and
what You've called me to be. When I look to You as my
example, I realize meek doesn't mean being weak. It means
being obedient to Abba God. Trusting Him to handle what I
cannot. Being quiet and patient while He works out His will
and way. And being gentle with others. In this view, being
meek carries strength with it. You Yourself, the Son of God
and my King, rode a simple donkey through the throng the
Sunday before Your death. I want to have that meekness,
that trust in Abba God. Show me the way there so that
I too can find the joy that comes with quiet strength. Amen.

Day 99

THE RIGHT SHORE

They saw Jesus walking on the sea and approaching the boat. And they were afraid (terrified). But Jesus said to them, It is I; be not afraid! [I Am; stop being frightened!] Then they were quite willing and glad for Him to come into the boat. And now the boat went at once to the land they had steered toward. [And immediately they reached the shore toward which they had been slowly making their way.]

JOHN 6:19–21 AMPC

Sometimes, Lord, I wonder why I'm getting nowhere with a project, task, challenge, or situation. I feel as if I'm out on a stormy sea, unable to see past the wind and waves, that all my rowing, all my efforts to move things forward are coming to naught. And then I realize I haven't invited You into my plans. For some reason, I've left You out of my equation. So here I am, Lord, letting You into my plan. Here's what I'm steering toward. Now that we're together on this, I can ride on in peace and make my way to the right shore with You. Amen.

Day 100

A PEACEFUL SLEEP

When you are on your bed, look into your hearts and be quiet. Give the gifts that are right and good, and trust in the Lord. Many are asking, "Who will show us any good?" . . . You have filled my heart with more happiness than they have when there is much grain and wine. I will lie down and sleep in peace. O Lord, You alone keep me safe.

PSALM 4:4–8 NLV

It's so hard to have joy, Lord, when I don't get enough sleep at night. So I'm asking for Your help. When I'm in bed, help me commune with my heart. To review my day and ask Your forgiveness for anything I may have done or said that I shouldn't have. To count my blessings, one by one. Then, Lord, help me to quiet my body and soul in Your presence. Fill me with all the joy I need to find peace of heart and mind. For only then, with You and Your blessings covering me, with Your protection and arms around me, will I find the rest I need and the safety I crave. In Jesus' name I pray, amen.

Day 101

UNBROKEN TRANQUILITY

*When the Lamb broke the seventh lock, there was not
a sound in heaven for about one-half hour. Then I saw
the seven angels standing before God. They were given
seven horns. Another angel came and stood at the altar.
He held a cup made of gold full of special perfume.
He was given much perfume so he could mix it in with
the prayers of those who belonged to God. Their prayers
were put on the altar made of gold before the throne.*

REVELATION 8:1–3 NLV

. . . .

There is something so precious, Lord, about being in silence
before You. For in this stillness, I find unbroken tranquility.
A time to reflect on the awesomeness of the joy experienced
in Your presence. Here I feel Your light, the warmth of
Your love and compassion, Your mercy and comfort. It is
here, in these unbroken moments with You, that I sit in
wonder and anticipation, not knowing what to expect, yet
expecting nothing but good. Your peace calms my heart,
soul, spirit, body, and mind. Time stands still as I stand
with You. Then little by little, my prayers and praises rise
up to You. And I find Your heavenly joy. In Jesus' name,
I await. Amen.

Day 102

SPIRITUAL NOURISHMENT

He opened His mouth and taught them, saying. . . Blessed
and fortunate and happy and spiritually prosperous (in
that state in which the born-again child of God enjoys
His favor and salvation) are those who hunger and
thirst for righteousness (uprightness and right standing
with God), for they shall be completely satisfied! . . .
The disciples urged Him saying, Rabbi, eat something.
But He assured them, I have food (nourishment) to
eat of which you know nothing and have no idea.
MATTHEW 5:2, 6; JOHN 4:31–32 AMPC

Abba God, only You can fill this longing I have inside, this God-shaped hole within me. I ache to hear Your voice, see Your face, feel Your touch. I hunger and thirst for all You have to give me, for all You are holding for me. I know You're just waiting to give me everything I need. So help me, Lord, to let go of all things that are not of You—worries, fears, what-ifs, possessions, deadlines, stress, and anxieties. For when I empty myself of all but You and Your Word, I know I'll find the nourishment that brings with it all the joy my spirit craves. Amen.

EVEN BETTER

Fear not, for I have redeemed you [ransomed you by paying a price instead of leaving you captives]; I have called you by your name; you are Mine. When you pass through the waters, I will be with you, and through the rivers, they will not overwhelm you. When you walk through the fire, you will not be burned or scorched, nor will the flame kindle upon you. For I am the Lord your God, the Holy One of Israel, your Savior.
ISAIAH 43:1–3 AMPC

. . . .

Oh Lord, You give me such peace of mind. When I am afraid, You tell me to "fear not" because You've redeemed me, even though it cost the sacrifice of Your Child. And You continue to reach out for me, willing and longing to help me. You've even called me by name, claiming ownership of me—mind, body, and soul. Even better, You've promised to stick with me through times of fire and times of rain. And all because You love me, all because You want me in Your world, Your presence. Alleluia, amen!

Day 104

REVIVED AGAIN

Be to me a rock of refuge, to which I may continually come. . . . O God, from my youth you have taught me, and I still proclaim your wondrous deeds. So even to old age and gray hairs, O God, do not forsake me, until I proclaim your might to another generation. . . . You. . .will revive me again. . . . My lips will shout for joy, when I sing praises to you.
PSALM 71:3, 17–18, 20, 23 ESV

. . . .

You have never failed me, Lord. When I've needed Your help, You have always come through for me. Time and time again, You have worked wonders in my life. Since I was a child in the faith, You have been my rock of refuge. So do not leave me now, Lord. Help me to grow more and more like Your Son, Jesus. Give me the words to tell others of Your power, love, compassion, and strength. Renew me. Fill me with Your light. Work in me for Your good and glory. And I will shout for joy as I sing Your praises for Your glory. Amen.

ONE CALL AWAY

"'Call to me and I will answer you. I'll tell you
marvelous and wondrous things that you could
never figure out on your own.' . . . Working a true
healing inside and out. . .life brimming with
blessings. I'll restore everything that was lost. . . .
I'll build everything back as good as new. . . .
[It] will be a center of joy and praise."
JEREMIAH 33:3, 6–7, 9 MSG

. . . .

When things look irredeemable and dark, when all seems
lost, I have one hope, Lord: You. You have said that if
I call out to You, You'll hear and answer me. You'll tell
me all kinds of things I don't know. You'll explain all the
mysteries, tell me things I could never figure out in my
own finite mind. And then You'll fix what seems unfixable.
You'll heal my life, my world, from the inside out. My life
will be running over with so many blessings. You'll bring
back everything I've lost, make my world as good as new.
Because of that promise, I have hope that my joy and
praises to You are one call away. In Jesus' name, amen.

NEVER FORGOTTEN

Sing for joy, O heavens! Be glad, O earth! Break out into songs of joy, O mountains! For the Lord has comforted His people. . . . "Can a woman forget her nursing child? Can she have no pity on the son to whom she gave birth? Even these may forget, but I will not forget you. See, I have marked your names on My hands. Your walls are always before Me."

ISAIAH 49:13, 15–16 NLV

. . . .

Oh Lord, with You in my life, I need not worry about being passed over! For You are always with me. You will never forget me—just like a nursing mother will never forget her newborn. But You go even further by tattooing my name on Your hands! Thank You for leading me, protecting me before and behind, providing for me, healing me, showering me with blessings, and fighting those who threaten me. Your pervading presence in my life gives me such joy. Such peace of mind. You chase all my blues away. Thank You, Father God, for never leaving me behind. Because of You, I break out, singing songs of joy. In Jesus' name I praise You. Amen.

Day 107

UNSHAKEN

God is our safe place and our strength. He is always our help when we are in trouble. So we will not be afraid, even if the earth is shaken and the mountains fall into the center of the sea, and even if its waters go wild with storm and the mountains shake with its action. . . . God is in the center of her. She will not be moved. God will help her when the morning comes.
PSALM 46:1–3, 5 NLV

. . . .

You, Lord, are my center. Because You are standing solidly within me, I need not be moved. Nothing can shake me unless I allow it. Help me to keep this in mind, Lord. To remember that I have You as my source of strength, courage, and hope. You alone are my safe place. You are always there when I'm in trouble no matter what that trouble is. So I will not be afraid. Even if the earth is shaken to its core, I will stand strong. I will remember I am Your child, Your daughter. And that You will help me when the daylight breaks and beyond. Amen.

Day 108

LOVING CARE NOT SPARED

He opened His mouth and taught them, saying: . . .
Blessed (happy, to be envied, and spiritually prosperous—
with life-joy and satisfaction in God's favor and salvation,
regardless of their outward conditions) are the merciful,
for they shall obtain mercy! . . . As Jesus passed on from
there, two blind men followed Him, shouting loudly,
Have pity and mercy on us, Son of David! . . . Then He
touched their eyes. . .and their eyes were opened.
MATTHEW 5:2, 7; 9:27, 29–30 AMPC

I thank You, Jesus, for Your mercy. Your loving-kindness and Your care for me seem to have no end. While You were here on earth, You were constantly reaching out to help others. And Your Word tells me that if I am kind and loving to others, caring for them as You care for me, I will find myself loved and cared for. Help me to do so, Lord. To reach out in love to those who need it. To care for those who are careless. For when I do, the blessings and joy will flow, eyes will be opened, and hearts touched for You. In Jesus' name, amen.

THE HOLY TAKEOVER

My grace is enough; it's all you need. My strength comes into its own in your weakness. Once I heard that, I was glad to let it happen. I quit focusing on the handicap and began appreciating the gift. It was a case of Christ's strength moving in on my weakness. Now I take limitations in stride, and with good cheer, these limitations that cut me down to size—abuse, accidents, opposition, bad breaks. I just let Christ take over! And so the weaker I get, the stronger I become.

2 CORINTHIANS 12:9–10 MSG

Lord, You certainly have a way of turning my life upside down. When I'm feeling weak because of some calamity, illness, abuse, or a "bad break," You come out in full force. As I become weaker and weaker, unable to handle things on my own, You show up in a big way and work through me. In fact, You make things perfect! So I'm making a point to stop focusing on what's wrong and to start focusing on You. I'm going to stay joyful no matter what limitations assail me. I'm going to step aside and let *You* take over. In that way, the weaker I get, the stronger in You I'll become. Amen.

PURE LIGHT AND JOY

You are the Lord Most High over all the earth. . . .
Let those who love the Lord hate what is bad.
For He keeps safe the souls of His faithful ones. He takes
them away from the hand of the sinful. Light is spread
like seed for those who are right and good, and joy
for the pure in heart. Be glad in the Lord, you who
are right and good. Give thanks to His holy name.
PSALM 97:9–12 NLV

Lord, help my love of You keep me away from things that are not good for me. For anything that is not good is not of You, God. Keep my soul safe from the evil that presents itself in the physical and spiritual worlds. Hide me under Your banner of love so that the sinful cannot reach me. Shine Your light along my way, so that I will not stumble upon Your path. Help me to continue to walk in Jesus' steps, the right and good way, for there alone will I find the deep joy I seek and the pure love I crave from You. In Jesus' name I pray, amen.

Day 111

NEWS BEARER

*How beautiful on the mountains are the feet of him
who brings good news, who tells of peace and brings
good news of happiness, who tells of saving power,
and says to Zion, "Your God rules!" . . . You will not
go out in a hurry. You will not leave as if you were
running for your lives. For the Lord will go before you.
And the God of Israel will keep watch behind you.*
ISAIAH 52:7, 12 NLV

. . . .

I've heard Your good news, Lord. I've heard of Your Son's
strength, peace, love, and saving power. Now, Lord, make
me a messenger of Your good news. Make me a light that
helps others find their way to You, the God of all, the King
who reigns over all. And as I continue to make my way
to You, to walk down the path You have put before me,
I will not hurry. For I am confident You are going before me,
paving my way. And You are walking behind me, guarding
me from the rear. Lord, make my feet beautiful for You
as I spread Your joy and share Your news with all. Amen.

Day 112

OPEN DOORS

*Though the disciples were behind closed doors for
fear of the Jews, Jesus came and stood among them
and said, Peace to you! So saying, He showed them
His hands and His side. And when the disciples saw
the Lord, they were filled with joy (delight, exultation,
ecstasy, rapture). Then Jesus said to them again,
Peace to you! . . . And having said this, He breathed
on them and said to them, Receive the Holy Spirit!*
JOHN 20:19–22 AMPC

Lord Jesus, sometimes this world leaves me cowering in
fear, afraid to move forward. In defense, I put up walls
and barriers, hoping my safety will lie there. But You, Lord,
open all doors and come shining through. Your words and
Your blessing of peace draw me out of my fear and into
You. Seeing Your face, I am filled with joy once more.
Reminded of who You are, what You've suffered for me,
I am renewed, made whole again. Your peace and Spirit
surround me, cocooning me in Your grace, mercy, love, and
presence. Breathe on me, Jesus. Strengthen my heart, soul,
and mind as I abide and rest in You. Amen.

LET BE, BE STILL, AND KNOW

*The Lord of hosts is with us; the God of Jacob is our
Refuge (our Fortress and High Tower). . . . Let be and
be still, and know (recognize and understand) that I
am God. I will be exalted among the nations! I will
be exalted in the earth! The Lord of hosts is with us;
the God of Jacob is our Refuge (our High Tower and
Stronghold). Selah [pause, and calmly think of that]!*

Psalm 46:7, 10–11 ampc

. . . .

I awaken with the words *be still and know* echoing in my
mind. Reading them, hearing them, a supernatural calm
drifts down upon me. Knowing that my God, the gentle
Shepherd who leads me, is also my high tower, impenetrable fortress, eternal refuge, and lion tamer fills me with
delight and wonder. I marvel at how an almighty God can
also be so gentle, how a Master can be a servant. And then
I hear You call my name. I turn, and there You are with
me. Filled with Your presence, I let everything go. I empty
my body of all tension and my mind of all thoughts but
these: *Let be, be still, and know that I am God.* And soon
Your surpassing peace reigns. Amen.

Day 114

BLESSINGS OF GOODNESS

The king shall have joy in Your strength, O Lord;
and in Your salvation how greatly shall he rejoice!
You have given him his heart's desire, and have not
withheld the request of his lips. For You meet him with the
blessings of goodness. . . . You have made him exceedingly
glad with Your presence. For the king trusts in the Lord,
and through the mercy of the Most High he shall not be moved.
PSALM 21:1–3, 6–7 NKJV

It's Your strength and power, Lord, that get me through each day, that bring me great joy. Every day You shower me with blessings, giving me what I desire, answering my prayers. All that is good comes from Your hand. And for all these things I thank You, Lord. Yet no blessing, no good thing You place in my life gives me more joy than Your very presence. For it is my trust that You will come when I call, my faith that You are here by my side right now, and my belief in Your loving-kindness that keep me steady, able to walk, able to serve You. In Jesus' name, amen.

Day 115

SOMETHING BETTER

You had loving-pity for those who were in prison.
You had joy when your things were taken away from you.
For you knew you would have something better in heaven
which would last forever. Do not throw away your trust,
for your reward will be great. You must be willing to wait
without giving up. After you have done what God wants
you to do, God will give you what He promised you.
HEBREWS 10:34–36 NLV

. . . .

There are times, Lord, when I fear my heart is more attached to the treasures I have on earth than those I have in heaven. Help me change that up, Lord. Help me to have love for people, not things. To be happy whether I have little or lots. To have joy even during times of loss, knowing something better than "things" awaits me in heaven. Also, Lord, give me the patience to wait for You to move in my life and the power to do what You would have me do. For when I'm walking Your way, I know that the fulfillment of promises You've made to me will follow. Amen.

Day 116

PURE HEART VISION

He opened His mouth and taught them, saying: . . .
Blessed (happy, enviably fortunate, and spiritually
prosperous. . .) are the pure in heart, for they shall
see God! . . . . No man has ever seen God at any time;
the only unique Son. . .Who is in the bosom [in the intimate
presence] of the Father, He has declared Him [He has
revealed Him and brought Him out where He can be seen].
MATTHEW 5:2, 8; JOHN 1:18 AMPC

Only by looking at and through You, Jesus, can I see God in all His goodness, strength, power, mercy, and loving-kindness. Yet to be able to see God completely, to actually be able to fully enter into His presence, my heart and mind must be right with You. So help me, Lord, get and keep my heart pure. Help me focus my thoughts on You, Jesus. To steep myself in Your Word. To walk in Your way. To stay on Your path. To forgive as You have forgiven. And to follow Your lead in all I do and say, all I think and pray. In Your name, amen.

Day 117

THE SECRET OF FACING EVERY SITUATION

Not that I am implying that I was in any personal want, for I have learned how to be content (satisfied to the point where I am not disturbed or disquieted) in whatever state I am. I know how to be abased and live humbly in straitened circumstances, and I know also how to enjoy plenty and live in abundance. I have learned in any and all circumstances the secret of facing every situation.
PHILIPPIANS 4:11–12 AMPC

. . . .

Help me get it through my head, Lord, that I, by myself, cannot meet my own needs. That only through You can I find the true contentment, joy, and peace I crave. Instead of trying to come up with my own solutions or thinking I know better than You, I'm going to trust You for everything—big and small. I'm going to allow You into every facet of my life. And I'm going to be satisfied with who I am, what I have, and where I am as I keep my eyes on You. For I know You do all things well and in Your own time. In You, I am content with all. Amen.

ROAD TO WISDOM

Trust in the Lord with all your heart, and do not trust in your own understanding. Agree with Him in all your ways, and He will make your paths straight. Do not be wise in your own eyes. Fear the Lord and turn away from what is sinful. It will be healing to your body and medicine to your bones. . . . Happy is the man who finds wisdom, and the man who gets understanding.

PROVERBS 3:5–8, 13 NLV

. . . .

This world seems to be getting more and more complicated every day. There are so many choices one can make, so many roads one can take. I'm sometimes confused, Lord, not sure what to do, which path to choose. Give me the wisdom I need to walk the right way. I'm trusting You and Your wisdom, not my own. I'm going to agree with You on everything. I'm turning myself over to You, knowing that in Your wisdom lies my path to true and lasting joy. Under Your direction will I find the true remedy I need. Amen.

Day 119

PEACE OF KNOWLEDGE

*I have learned in any and all circumstances the secret of
facing every situation, whether well-fed or going hungry,
having a sufficiency and enough to spare or going without
and being in want. I have strength for all things in Christ
Who empowers me [I am ready for anything and equal
to anything through Him Who infuses inner strength
into me; I am self-sufficient in Christ's sufficiency].*
PHILIPPIANS 4:12–13 AMPC

. . . .

No matter what's happening in my life, Lord, I know that
because of You, I'll never want for anything. For I belong
to You, the Master Creator, maintainer, and sustainer of
all things. And because I'm Yours, everything I see around
me reminds me of You, Your power, Your beauty, and Your
love. All I have, want, and require is in You, from You, and
through You. Because I live in You and Your Son, I have it
all, including strength to do, think, or say what You would
have me do, think, or say. Through Your Son I'm ready
for anything because He is my everything, my security,
strength, and peace. In Jesus' name, amen.

PEACEMAKER
AND MAINTAINER

He opened His mouth and taught them, saying: . . .
Blessed (enjoying enviable happiness, spiritually
prosperous—with life-joy and satisfaction in God's favor
and salvation, regardless of their outward conditions)
are the makers and maintainers of peace, for they
shall be called the sons of God! . . . In Christ Jesus,
you. . .have been brought near. For He is [Himself]
our peace (our bond of unity and harmony).
MATTHEW 5:2, 9; EPHESIANS 2:13–14 AMPC

In this contentious world, Lord, I want to be a maker and maintainer of peace. To bring harmony instead of havoc wherever I go, whatever I do, whomever I meet. But I need help, Lord. Lots of it. Tell me when to remain silent and when to speak. And if I am to speak, give me the words You would have me say. You are my peace, Lord. Now mold me into someone who can bring peace to others. When people see the calmness I bear without, as well as the harmony I keep within, may they see me as a blessed and happy daughter of God. In Jesus' name I pray, amen.

Day 121
DO NOT LET

Do not let your hearts be troubled (distressed, agitated).
You believe in and adhere to and trust in and rely on
God; believe in and adhere to and trust in and rely also
on Me. . . . Believe Me that I am in the Father and the
Father in Me; or else believe Me for the sake of the [very]
works themselves. [If you cannot trust Me, at least let
these works that I do in My Father's name convince you.]
JOHN 14:1, 11 AMPC

. . . .

Lord, I'm having trouble maintaining my peace. That may
be because my attention has shifted. For during these
tumultuous times, I'm more focused on the world's troubles
than I am on You. And that's never a good tack to take.
So help me get back on the right line, Lord. Bring back to
my mind all the things You have done—in history and in
my life. Show me the world through Your eyes. Guide me
in how to make my priorities those of heaven, not earth.
Remind me, God, of who You are—the Father I trust, the
Son I lean on, and the Spirit I seek. Amen.

Day 122

AN EDEN-LIKE TRANSFORMATION

"All you who are serious about right living and committed to seeking God. Ponder the rock from which you were cut. . . . Abraham, your father, and Sarah, who bore you. Think of it! One solitary man when I called him, but once I blessed him, he multiplied. Likewise I, God, will comfort Zion. . . . I'll transform her dead ground into Eden. . .the garden of God, a place filled with exuberance and laughter, thankful voices and melodic songs."
ISAIAH 51:1–3 MSG

You, Lord God, can do anything. And You *will* do anything for those serious about living the way You want them to live. To those committed to seeking You each and every day. From Abraham to Jesus, You have blessed Your people by fulfilling their most ardent desires. I want to be as serious about living right as Abraham was. I want to be as committed to seeking You as Jesus was. Then You will turn my world—within and without—into a garden of Eden, a place where laughter is heard, love is spread, and prayers of gratitude roll off our lips. Transform me, Lord, in Jesus' name. Amen.

Day 123

A PLACE FOR YOU

*In My Father's house there are many dwelling places
(homes). If it were not so, I would have told you; for I am
going away to prepare a place for you. And when (if) I go
and make ready a place for you, I will come back again and
will take you to Myself, that where I am you may be also.
And [to the place] where I am going, you know the way.*
JOHN 14:2–4 AMPC

. . . .

I like it, Lord, that You're a man with a plan. That You
have been with me since the beginning, are still with me
now, and will be with me in the future. Yet it's not just
that truth that keeps me calm and content. It's the fact
that Father God has a nice home waiting for me. And that
You have gone ahead to prepare that place for me—for me
alone. To me, Lord, this isn't just a place in the future but
a place I can visit now. A place where I can be with You
alone. A place of peace, comfort, and hope. A place of light
and love. A place of never-ending choruses of amens. In
Jesus' name, amen.

Day 124

RIGHT FOR LIFE

He began to teach them, saying, . . . "Those who have it
very hard for doing right are happy, because the holy
nation of heaven is theirs. You are happy when people act
and talk in a bad way to you and make it very hard for
you and tell bad things and lies about you because you
trust in Me." . . . Christ. . .never sinned and yet He died
for us who have sinned. . .so He might bring us to God.
MATTHEW 5:2, 10–11; 1 PETER 3:18 NLV

. . . .

Lord Jesus, there's no way I can ever repay You for all
You've done for me. You, who never sinned, died so that
I, a sinner, might live. You put up with the leers and jeers
of the ungodly. You put up with the lies and the pain of
unjust accusers. What You've gone through and done for
me inspires me, Lord, to take this new life You've given me
and live it for You—no matter what others say about me or
do to me. Because, as I live for You and trust in You, I gain
Your kingdom of heaven—and all the joy and happiness that
come with it. Thank You, Lord, for bringing me to God. In
Your name I pray, amen.

Day 125

LAMBS IN ARMS

*"Look! Your God!" Look at him! God, the Master, comes
in power, ready to go into action. He is going to pay
back his enemies and reward those who have loved him.
Like a shepherd, he will care for his flock, gathering
the lambs in his arms, hugging them as he carries
them, leading the nursing ewes to good pasture.*
ISAIAH 40:10–11 MSG

Lord, You are the giver, the bringer, the gatherer, the lover, the leader of life. You are the source of all power and light. And to the ones who love You, You come in power and take action. You, my champion and Good Shepherd, care for me in every stage of my life—from lamb to ewe and all the phases in between. And as You care for and love me, Your light and warmth cover me, enclose me, protect and caress me. I find my true peace, my haven, when I imagine Your strong and steady arms embracing me. Continue to lead me along Your pathway. Ease me into Your will and desire. Show me how to maintain my peace in Your pasture. My eyes will continue to look to You, my God, my Master, my Shepherd. Amen.

Day 126

LOOKING AT YOU

"O give thanks to the Lord. Call upon His name. Let the people know what He has done. Sing to Him. Sing praises to Him. Tell of all His great works. Have joy in His holy name. Let the heart of those who look to the Lord be glad. Look to the Lord and ask for His strength. Look to Him all the time. Remember His great works which He has done."
1 CHRONICLES 16:8–12 NLV

• •

Today, God, I want to thank You for calling me. I praise Your name in remembrance of all You have done for Your people—from the parting of the Red Sea, to making the earth stand still, to sending a host of angels to protect us, to sending Your Son to bring us back to You, heart, body, mind, and soul. You have breathed Your life into me, Lord. And to You, my source, I look at all times—for guidance, protection, love, mercy, forgiveness, strength, and power. In Your name and works, in Your lovely face, I find all the joy I desire. Here's looking at You, Lord, today and forever. Amen.

Day 127

LOST AND FOUND

*I would have been lost in my troubles if Your Law
had not been my joy. I will never forget Your Word
for by it You have given me new life. I am Yours.
Save me, for I have looked to Your Law. . . .
You are my hiding place and my battle-covering.
I put my hope in Your Word. . . . I am made happy
by Your Word, like one who finds great riches.*
PSALM 119:92–94, 114, 162 NLV

. . . .

Lord, when I'm desperate, when I see no way out of my
problems, when I'm overwhelmed with sorrow, I seek You
and Your Word. Save me, Lord. Be my hiding place. Cover
me with Your shadow so that I can rest and recover. Then,
when I can once again rise in Your power, show me the
way out, the way back to the joy that Your pathway and
presence bring. I am Yours, Lord. All my hope lies in You
and Your wisdom. I come to You lost, and by Your Word
I'm found. Your Word is the treasure I seek, and it holds
the promises of all my tomorrows. Word by word, I find
my peace and my way back to You. In Jesus' name, amen.

Day 128

NEVER SEEN, YET BELIEVED

*His disciples were again in the house, and Thomas
was with them. Jesus came, though they were
behind closed doors, and stood among them and
said, Peace to you! . . . Because you have seen Me,
Thomas, do you now believe (trust, have faith)?
Blessed and happy and to be envied are those
who have never seen Me and yet have believed
and adhered to and trusted and relied on Me.*

JOHN 20:26, 29 AMPC

It's true, Jesus. I have never seen You physically. Yet unlike doubting Thomas, I believe in You. Between You and me are no closed doors. As soon as You stand beside me, I feel Your peace and joy, Your strength and power. You call me blessed and happy because I believe in, rely on, and trust in You without ever having seen You. And I *am*! For You are my way to the Father. You are the truth I need. You are the life I seek. I am nowhere without You. So stick close to me, Lord, as I stick close to You. Continually bless me as I follow in Your footsteps. Help me to recognize that no matter what each day brings, my path, my purpose, and my joy lie in You. Amen.

Day 129

DESIRED HAVEN

Some go down to the sea and travel over it in ships. . . .
Then they cry to the Lord in their trouble, and He brings
them out of their distresses. He hushes the storm to
a calm and to a gentle whisper, so that the waves of
the sea are still. Then the men are glad because of the
calm, and He brings them to their desired haven.
PSALM 107:23, 28–30 AMPC

Troubles are causing a storm within and without, Lord. My calm has been shaken, my thoughts disrupted. I'm truly not sure what to do. And then, in desperation, I cry out to You. Immediately I feel relief, just in sharing my troubles with You, the one who knows me best. You hush the storm within, and I feel a gentle calm come over me. I can now hear Your whisper where a howling gale once surrounded me. The tumultuous waves have even become still. In this glad state, this state of peace, I feel sane and safe once more. You have brought me back to You, my desired haven in the best and worst of times. For no time is wasted in Your peace, Your presence. My God, You are my shelter from all storms. Amen.

Day 130

LIFTING UP

I will lift You up, O Lord, for You have lifted me up. You have not let those who hate me stand over me in joy. O Lord my God, I cried to You for help and You healed me. O Lord, You have brought me up from the grave. You have kept me alive, so that I will not go down into the deep. Sing praise to the Lord, all you who belong to Him. Give thanks to His holy name.

PSALM 30:1–4 NLV

. . . .

It's only right that I should lift You up, Lord, because You've certainly lifted me up. When I first awoke, I wondered what this day would bring. But before my thoughts went too far, I looked to You and into Your Word. There I found how You continually help and heal me. You give me new life each and every day. You and Your light are what keep me from sliding into that dark abyss. So, today, Lord, I'm praising Your name, singing songs of love to You. I thank You for always being there; rescuing me when I'm in danger; walking with me through the storms; holding me tight in the night hours; showing me the pathway of life. . .in You. Amen.

Day 131

MOVING IN

*"I'm in my Father, and you're in me, and I'm in you.
The person who knows my commandments and keeps
them, that's who loves me. And the person who loves
me will be loved by my Father, and I will love him
and make myself plain to him. . . . If anyone loves me,
he will carefully keep my word and my Father will
love him—we'll move right into the neighborhood!"*
JOHN 14:20–21, 23 MSG

. . . .

I have a sense of peace within me each time I think of
You, Jesus. I feel so complete knowing You are in God,
I'm in You, and You're in me. Because that means that no
matter where I am or what I'm doing, I'm never alone.
I always have someone with me who can give me wisdom,
lift me up, shelter me from harm, and love me like no
other. The last on that list is the most important, Lord,
because this world can be such a loveless, unforgiving
place. Fortunately for me, Lord, You loved me before I
even knew You. That's a love to treasure, to count on, to
rest in. Thank You. Amen.

SWIMMING IN SUCCESS

Simon Peter said to them, "I am going fishing." The others
said, "We will go with you." . . . That night they caught
no fish. Early in the morning Jesus stood on the shore
of the lake. . . . He said to them, "Put your net over the
right side of the boat. Then you will catch some fish."
They put out the net. They were not able to pull it in
because it was so full of fish. . . . There were 153 big fish.
JOHN 21:3–4, 6, 11 NLV

Jesus, I love this story of how Your discouraged disciples
have caught no fish. Then You come along, tell them what
to do, and they end up catching 153! But the best part is
that when Peter realizes it's You, he jumps into the water
and swims to Your side! What an expression of joy! That's
how I feel, Lord. When I'm discouraged, stuck, out of ideas,
Your voice comes through. I follow it, and the next thing
I know, I'm swimming in success, rushing joyfully to Your
side to share my bounty with You! Thank You, Lord, for
all the victories You supply, to Your glory. In Jesus' name
I pray, amen.

IN YOUR MIDST

The King of Israel, even the Lord [Himself], is in the
midst of you. . . . Fear not. . . . Let not your hands
sink down or be slow and listless. The Lord your
God is in the midst of you, a Mighty One, a Savior
[Who saves]! He will rejoice over you with joy;
He will rest [in silent satisfaction] and in His love
He will be silent and make no mention [of past sins,
or even recall them]; He will exult over you with singing.
ZEPHANIAH 3:15–17 AMPC

. . . .

It amazes me, Lord, that You, the King of kings, the Master planner, the Lord of creation, are right here in my midst. That gives me courage to face what lies ahead, to step out of my comfort zone. It gives me the strength I need to say and do what You would have me say and do. Even more amazing is that You are happy with me and love me! And when I make a wrong move or turn from Your way, You will not just forgive me but *forget* my mistakes. In fact, You will never mention them. All this, Lord, makes me as joyful in You as You are in me! Amen!

Day 134

DRESSED WITH JOY

Sing praise to the Lord, all you who belong to Him. . . .
His favor is for life. Crying may last for a night,
but joy comes with the new day. . . . Show me loving-
kindness. O Lord, be my Helper. You have turned my
crying into dancing. You have taken off my clothes
made from hair, and dressed me with joy. So my
soul may sing praise to You, and not be quiet.
PSALM 30:4–5, 10–12 NLV

. . . .

Sometimes, Lord, when I'm grieving over a loss, it's hard to even consider happiness. Yet a seed of joy can be found in the hope of Your Word. For You have said, "Crying may last for a night, but joy comes with the new day." On the down days, Lord, help me tap into that hope—that promise that on some day, at some point, I will once again find and experience joy. That You will turn my crying into dancing, take off my black mourning suit and dress me with joy. In the meantime, help me write this promise on my heart so that I can, in some way, bring this knowledge to mind when the time comes and praise You amid the pain. Amen.

Day 135

REPLENISH

Lift up your eyes on high and see! Who has created these? . . . Have you not known? Have you not heard? The everlasting God, the Lord, the Creator of the ends of the earth, does not faint or grow weary; there is no searching of His understanding. He gives power to the faint and weary, and to him who has no might He increases strength [causing it to multiply and making it to abound].

ISAIAH 40:26, 28–29 AMPC

. . . .

I know who You are, Lord. You're the Creator of all. The one who holds, maintains, and sustains the entire world. I have known this. But sometimes, almost unknowingly, I forget who You are. . .and, for that matter, who *I* am! I get so caught up in the day-to-day machinations in this world that I put You and Your power, strength, and knowledge to the side and tap into my resources alone. That's when I get into trouble. So here I am, Lord, faint and weary. Replenish me with Your peace, power, and strength. Shower me with Your wisdom. And help me keep my mind on You every moment of the day. Amen.

Day 136

YOUR PRAYER
HAS BEEN HEARD

*The angel said to him, "Zacharias, do not be afraid.
Your prayer has been heard. Your wife Elizabeth will give
birth to a son. You are to name him John. You will be glad
and have much joy. Many people will be happy because
he is born. He will be great in the sight of the Lord. . . .
Even from his birth, he will be filled with the Holy Spirit."*
LUKE 1:13–15 NLV

. . . .

I love Your Word, Lord. For it not only gives me a great
picture of You, but its stories prove that You are forever
working in people's lives. That You *do* answer prayer.
That I should never give up praying for something. No
matter how many years go by. No matter how old I get.
No matter how seemingly impossible my request becomes.
I will never lose hope nor forget that You hear me when
I pray. So here I am, Lord, once more coming to You with
the same request. Give me the joy of Your answer, Lord.
I await Your reply, praising Your name, knowing my prayer
has been heard by the doer of the impossible. Amen.

Day 137

BOOK ON LIVING

Everything's falling apart on me, GOD; put me together again with your Word. Adorn me with your finest sayings, GOD; teach me your holy rules. My life is as close as my own hands, but I don't forget what you have revealed. . . . I inherited your book on living; it's mine forever—what a gift! And how happy it makes me! I concentrate on doing exactly what you say—I always have and always will.
PSALM 119:107–109, 111–112 MSG

. . . .

Just when I feel as if I'm losing my way, Lord, I run to Your Book. Use Your Word to put me back together, Lord. To get me back on the right track, living Your way. Teach me what I need to learn so I don't backtrack or take a wrong turn. Help me follow Your rules of life so that I can stop worrying and begin rejoicing! So that I can have the promise of Your peace, love, strength, and power. Help me focus on You and Your way so I won't lose my way to You. And if I do make a mistake, Lord, gently lead me back to You, Your path, Your Son. In Jesus' name, amen.

Day 138

TREES OF THE WOODS

"The Lord made the heavens. Honor and great power are with Him. Strength and joy are in His place. . . . Let the heavens be glad. Let the earth be filled with joy. And let them say among the nations, 'The Lord rules!' Let the sea thunder, and all that is in it. Let the field be happy, and all that is in it. Then the trees of the woods will sing for joy before the Lord."

1 CHRONICLES 16:26–27, 31–33 NLV

. . . .

What joy I find in the idea, in the fact that *You* are the grand Creator, Lord. That all I see—and all I do not see—has been made by Your hands. You are so great, powerful, and wonderful. All the strength and joy are where You are, and You are everywhere—even inside me as I abide in You. So I am rejoicing in that today, Lord. I trust in You, knowing You are in charge, controlling all things—places, people, and events! What a wonderful world You've created, one in which even the trees sing for joy before You! Be with me in this moment, Lord, as I take a nature walk and bask in the joy of Your making. Amen.

Day 139

WITHIN ME

Peace I leave with you; My [own] peace I now give and bequeath to you. Not as the world gives do I give to you. Do not let your hearts be troubled, neither let them be afraid. [Stop allowing yourselves to be agitated and disturbed; and do not permit yourselves to be fearful and intimidated and cowardly and unsettled.]
JOHN 14:27 AMPC

. . . .

It's strange reading the words "Stop allowing yourselves to be agitated and disturbed; and do not permit yourselves to be fearful," for I rarely consider that I have control over these things. And yet I do. I have a choice to make. I can allow the events of my day and my reactions to them to break my peace or not. I choose *not*. But I will need Your help, Lord, to hang on to Your peace—the one You left with me. The very peace You carried, have given to, and bequeathed to me. To hang on to Your peace, I'm going to spend more time in You, with You, attending to You— beginning today by reminding myself over and over again that the God of peace is within me. Amen.

Day 140

BLESSED BELIEF

Elizabeth. . .cried out. . . . Blessed (happy, to be envied)
is she who believed that there would be a fulfillment
of the things that were spoken to her from the Lord.
And Mary said, My soul magnifies and extols the Lord,
and my spirit rejoices in God my Savior, for He has looked
upon the low station and humiliation of His handmaiden
. . . . For He Who is almighty has done great things for me.
LUKE 1:41–42, 45–49 AMPC

I find my strength and joy, Lord, when I believe that You will do what Your Word says, when I have faith that You will keep Your promises to those who love You. Help me build up that belief and faith, Lord, more and more each day. Remind me each and every moment that through Your Word, strength, and power, I will not just find my way through this life, but my soul and spirit will rejoice over You in good times and not-so-good times. Help me base my life on the fact that You are doing great things for me and in me. In Jesus' name and power I pray, amen.

Day 141

THE GOOD SHEPHERD'S VOICE

*I am the Good Shepherd; and I know and recognize
My own, and My own know and recognize Me. . . .
The sheep that are My own hear and are listening
to My voice; and I know them, and they follow Me.
And I give them eternal life, and they shall never
lose it or perish throughout the ages. [To all eternity
they shall never by any means be destroyed.]*
JOHN 10:14, 27–28 AMPC

. . . .

There was just something about You, Jesus, that attracted
me. Perhaps it was Your truth in a world of half-truths.
Maybe it was the fact that You were both gentle and powerful. Or because You gave Your life for me. But then one
day I heard Your Word, Your *voice*—and I was truly and
forever hooked. Day after day, hour after hour, I kept
coming back to know, hear, and learn more about You
and Your ways. To this day, I can't seem to get enough.
My beloved Jesus, thank You for shepherding me. For
giving me eternal life. For giving my soul a craving for
Your voice. In Your name I pray, amen.

Day 142

THE WAY TO WISDOM

Happy is the man who finds wisdom, and the man who gets understanding. . . . She is worth more than stones of great worth. Nothing you can wish for compares with her. Long life is in her right hand. Riches and honor are in her left hand. Her ways are pleasing, and all her paths are peace. . . . Happy are all who hold her near.
PROVERBS 3:13, 15–18 NLV

. . . .

I want to search out Your knowledge, Lord. To understand what You want me to do, say, and think. Show me the path toward Your wisdom. May I pray for that more than anything else. For that is where I will find my direction. That is where I will find the answers I need. That is where I will discover the way You want me to go. So guide my reading of Your Word today, Lord. Show me what You want me to read. Tell me what You'd have me memorize and write upon my heart. Equip me with all I need to know so I can best serve You and find joy along the way. In Jesus' name I pray, amen.

Day 143

CONTINUAL BLESSING

I will bless the Lord at all times; His praise shall
continually be in my mouth. My life makes its boast in
the Lord; let the humble and afflicted hear and be glad.
O magnify the Lord with me, and let us exalt His name
together. I sought (inquired of) the Lord and required
Him [of necessity and on the authority of His Word],
and He heard me, and delivered me from all my fears.
PSALM 34:1–4 AMPC

No matter what is happening in my life, in my world, it is You, God, who I bless. For You hear me when I pray. Your love and kindness, Your compassion and mercy are all-encompassing. You make my life worth living. For life is no life at all when I'm tied up in troubles, distressed by doubts, and frantic with fears. So I come to You. When I enter Your presence, Your light obliterates my problems, indecisiveness, and insecurities. They fade into nothingness. And all that remain are Your light, warmth, and love. This is why I seek You, serve You, celebrate You, and surrender to You. In Jesus' name, amen.

Day 144

STARSTRUCK

The star [the wise men] had seen in the East went before them. It came and stopped over the place where the young Child was. When they saw the star, they were filled with much joy. They went into the house and found the young Child with Mary, His mother. Then they got down before Him and worshiped Him. They opened their bags of riches and gave Him gifts. . . . Then God spoke to them.
MATTHEW 2:9–12 NLV

. . . .

Jesus, I, like the wise men, followed the light and found You. What joy I discovered in You at our first meeting! What a journey it has been. What wonder I experience each day when I get down on my knees and worship You. I offer You my life, heart, body, mind, and soul. Yet if there are other gifts You would like me to hand over to You or share with others, please show me what they are. For my journey with You has just begun. I want to be Your hands and feet, serving You until I am with You on the other side. Speak to me, Lord. Show me the way to grow ever closer to You. In Your name I pray, amen.

Day 145

THE TRUE PATH

*If you've gotten anything at all out of following Christ,
if his love has made any difference in your life. . .
then do me a favor: Agree with each other, love each
other, be deep-spirited friends. Don't push your way
to the front; don't sweet-talk your way to the top.
Put yourself aside, and help others get ahead.
Don't be obsessed with getting your own advantage.
Forget yourselves long enough to lend a helping hand.*
PHILIPPIANS 2:1–4 MSG

. . . .

Sometimes, Lord, I feel like I'm living a life where it's all about me and what I want. Yet I know from Your Word and my experience that my true path to peace comes when I forget my own needs, plans, and desires—when I put myself aside long enough to help someone else. So help me do that, Lord. Help me find a way to agree with and love others. To be a friend who is sel*fless*, not sel*fish*. To look out not just for my own interests but also for the interest of others. To find a way to live in peace—within and without. In Jesus' name, amen.

Day 146

FRESH START

Count yourself lucky, how happy you must be—you get
a fresh start, your slate's wiped clean. Count yourself
lucky—God holds nothing against you and you're holding
nothing back from him. When I kept it all inside,
my bones turned to powder, my words became daylong
groans. . . . Then I let it all out; I said, "I'll come clean
about my failures to God." Suddenly the pressure was
gone—my guilt dissolved, my sin disappeared.

PSALM 32:1–3, 5 MSG

Lord, when I keep things from You, when I don't admit to You
(or myself) that I've done something wrong, it eats me up
inside. One wrongdoing piles up onto another and another,
and before I know it, I feel like I'm about to implode. So
here I am today, Lord, telling You not just the good things
I've done but the not-so-good. And I ask Your forgiveness
in the process. For then I will once again be able to tap
into joy, happy in God, counting myself lucky in the Lord
who not only removes my sin and guilt but makes them
disappear—*forever*! What a relief! In Jesus' name, amen.

Day 147

PEACE TO YOU!

Jesus came and stood among them and said, Peace to you! . . . Then Jesus said to them again, Peace to you! [Just] as the Father has sent Me forth, so I am sending you. And having said this, He breathed on them and said to them, Receive the Holy Spirit! . . . Eight days later His disciples were again in the house. . . . Jesus came, though they were behind closed doors, and stood among them and said, Peace to you!

JOHN 20:19, 21–22, 26 AMPC

. . . .

Nothing and no one can come between You and me, Jesus. Not even closed doors can keep You out. At one point, You walked through walls to get to Your followers. And I know You'll walk through more than walls to get to me—all so that I can hear Your message of peace. In this moment, Lord, come and stand beside me. Allow words of peace to come from Your lips, the airy essence of peace to cover me, the power of peace to pour down upon me. In Your name I pray and receive Your peace. Amen.

Day 148

THE GETAWAY

"Are you tired? Worn out? Burned out on religion?
Come to me. Get away with me and you'll recover
your life. I'll show you how to take a real rest.
Walk with me and work with me—watch how I do
it. Learn the unforced rhythms of grace. I won't lay
anything heavy or ill-fitting on you. Keep company
with me and you'll learn to live freely and lightly."
MATTHEW 11:28–30 MSG

Lord Jesus, joy is elusive at best when I'm not getting the rest I need—spiritually, mentally, emotionally, and physically. I'm worn out, burned out, and just plain tired. Exhausted. So I'm not just coming to You but limping to You. Please take this load of cares, worries, and woes off my back. Help me to give them up, to lay them at Your feet. Show me how to really rest. Teach me how to keep pace with and work with You. Help me walk in the "unforced rhythms of grace." Teach me how to live this life freely yet more fully. To bear Your light load so I may once more find joy. In Your name, amen.

Day 149

SAFE PLACE OF PEACE

When I was desperate, I called out, and God got me out of a tight spot. God's angel sets up a circle of protection around us while we pray. Open your mouth and taste, open your eyes and see—how good God is. Blessed are you who run to him. Worship God if you want the best; worship opens doors to all his goodness.

PSALM 34:6–9 MSG

. . . .

Even when I'm desperate, in dire straits, I still have peace. For You, God, always make a way even when I see no way. You see the benefits of all situations, the silver lining of every cloud. So when I call out, You do the next thing. You take the next step to help me get through whatever obstacle or problem is blocking my way. And You go even further by commanding Your angel to form a wall of protection around me, keeping me from all harm. So, with mouth and eyes open, I'm going to taste and see how good You are, Lord. As I run to You, knowing I'll reach my safe place in Your peace, I do so with exhilaration and joy, wondering how You're going to work things out. . .for me, in You. Amen.

Day 150

GROUNDED IN THE WORD

The seed which fell between rocks is like the person who receives the Word with joy as soon as he hears it. Its root is not deep and it does not last long. When troubles and suffering come because of the Word, he gives up and falls away. . . . The seed which fell on good ground is like the one who hears the Word and understands it. He gives much grain.
MATTHEW 13:20–21, 23 NLV

. . . .

I am so glad, Lord, that, at first hearing, I not only took in Your Word with joy but let it take root deep within me. But now sometimes on especially busy days, I find myself not making digging into Your Word a priority. Help me to change that, Lord. To look to You and Your Word before my day begins, before my feet hit the floor. Help me to go deeper and deeper into what You have to say. And help me grow in my prayer life. For I want to be one of Your good and faithful servants. To be so fruitful that I please You more than anyone or anything else, including myself. Amen.

PROMISED, PREDICTED, AND PROPOSED

This [very] night there stood by my side an angel of the God to Whom I belong and Whom I serve and worship, and he said, Do not be frightened, Paul! It is necessary for you to stand before Caesar; and behold, God has given you all those who are sailing with you. So keep up your courage, men, for I have faith (complete confidence) in God that it will be exactly as it was told me.

ACTS 27:23–25 AMPC

. . . .

God, throughout the ages, You have sent Your angels to watch over those who trust in You, the heirs of salvation. You've sent them as protectors, messengers, encouragers, and defenders. And, Lord, although I cannot see these supernatural beings, I know they, like You, are right here with me. That is why I can hang on to my peace and courage and use them to inspire peace and courage in others. Like Paul, no matter where I've come from, where I stand today, and what lies before me, I too can say, "I have faith (complete confidence) in God that it will be exactly as it was told me." Whatever You've promised, predicted, or proposed, dear Lord, will become reality. And so, I have peace knowing Your Word is my truth. In Jesus' name I pray, amen.

Day 152

A HIDING PLACE

Let all who are God-like pray to You while You
may be found, because in the floods of much water,
they will not touch him. You are my hiding place.
You keep me safe from trouble. . . . Many are the
sorrows of the sinful. But loving-kindness will be all
around the man who trusts in the Lord. Be glad in the
Lord and be full of joy, you who are right with God!
PSALM 32:6–7, 10–11 NLV

I am always amazed, Lord, at how You keep me out of troubles both seen and unseen. With You next to me, above me, below me, behind me, before me, and within me, I am truly safe no matter what comes my way. You, Lord, are my hiding place. To You I run. In You I trust. Surround me not only with Your power, strength, and presence but with all Your unfathomable loving-kindness as I praise You and pray to You. Keep my feet upon Your good path. And in You I will find not only joy, but everything I need. In Jesus' name, amen.

Day 153

BACK IN STEP

Acquaint now yourself with Him [agree with God and show yourself to be conformed to His will] and be at peace; by that [you shall prosper and great] good shall come to you. Receive, I pray you, the law and instruction from His mouth and lay up His words in your heart. If you return to the Almighty [and submit and humble yourself before Him], you will be built up.

JOB 22:21–23 AMPC

. . . .

I've been looking for peace, Lord. Yet it seems so elusive at times. And then I realize I am out of step with You and that may be a part of this disconnect I've been feeling. So here I am, Lord. I'm giving in to You, allowing my will to be aligned with Yours. As each minute, hour, and day passes, I'm going to be at peace, knowing You are once more my lead in this life. Your direction and words are going to be instilled in my heart so that I, in all ways—body, mind, and spirit—will be one with You, Your Son, and Your Spirit. In submitting to You, in serving You, in watching and waiting for You, I am renewed in, empowered by, and back in step with You. Amen.

Day 154

GOD-GIVEN JOY

*There is nothing better for a man than to eat and drink
and find joy in his work. I have seen that this also is
from the hand of God. For who can. . .find joy without
Him? For God has given wisdom and much learning
and joy to the person who is good in God's eyes.
But to the sinner He has given the work of. . .getting many
riches together to give to the one who pleases God.*
ECCLESIASTES 2:24–26 NLV

. . . .

Lord, some days I find myself not enjoying anything.
But now I realize that's because my thoughts and focus
are not on You. For only when I seek You first and bring
You to mind throughout my day do I find the joy I crave.
So remind me of Your presence, Lord, as I eat and drink—
and especially as I work. For I'm not really working for
my boss, my family, my church, my spouse, or my school.
No, I'm working for You. You are my source of true joy.
All I do, I do for You alone. For that work, those duties
are what truly last forever and ever. I pray and praise in
Jesus' name, amen.

Day 155

DIVINE IMPLANT

To everything there is a season, and a time for
every matter or purpose under heaven. . . . A time
to love and a time to hate, a time for war and a
time for peace. . . . He also has planted eternity
in men's hearts and minds [a divinely implanted
sense of a purpose working through the ages which
nothing under the sun but God alone can satisfy].
ECCLESIASTES 3:1, 8, 11 AMPC

. . . .

In You, Lord, there's a time for everything, for every purpose—to live and die, plant and reap, kill and heal, break
down and build up, weep and laugh, mourn and dance,
get and lose, cast away and gather, rend and sew, keep
silent and speak, love and hate, make war and make peace.
Knowing these things will happen in my life and accept-
ing those happenings as part and parcel of life helps me
keep peace in perspective. But even more so does the fact
that You've already planted within my heart and mind
a sense of foreverness, a divine sense of purpose that
only knowing, loving, and walking with You can satisfy.
So help me remember that there will be times both good
and bad—but all that really matters is my forever time
with You. In Jesus' name, amen.

Day 156

GIVING CHEERFULLY

He who sows sparingly will also reap sparingly,
and he who sows bountifully will also reap bountifully.
So let each one give as he purposes in his heart,
not grudgingly or of necessity; for God loves a cheerful
giver. And God is able to make all grace abound toward
you, that you, always having all sufficiency in all things,
may have an abundance for every good work.
2 CORINTHIANS 9:6–8 NKJV

When things are difficult financially, Lord, it's hard to give with a cheerful heart. But then I remember Your law: those who give little will get little; those who give much will get much. So help me keep that in mind, knowing that when I give cheerfully, no matter what my circumstances, I will reap cheerfully, beginning with a bountiful crop of joy. And I will also reap contentment. For as I give, You promise to supply me with everything I might need for all the work I'm doing in and for You. Ah, what a relief to live with the knowledge that as I bless others, I can count on You blessing me. Thank You, God, for all this and so much more. Amen.

Day 157

A HANDFUL OF PEACEFUL REPOSE

Luckier than the dead or the living is the person who has never even been, who has never seen the bad business that takes place on this earth. Then I observed all the work and ambition motivated by envy. What a waste! Smoke. And spitting into the wind. The fool sits back and takes it easy, his sloth is slow suicide. One handful of peaceful repose is better than two fistfuls of worried work.

ECCLESIASTES 4:3–6 MSG

. . . .

Help me, Lord, not to take on too many of the trials and troubles of others in addition to my own. Rein in my empathy or give me some other way to channel it, so that instead of worrying I can do something constructive to help people who are having trouble or are troubled. And when it comes to work, Lord, help me not to fret over it but to lean back on it and have peace abound around it. Remind me to send up a prayer every step of the way so that my work will be seen as Your handiwork, signed, sealed, and delivered by Your Spirit. Amen.

GRAND PLANS

Sing for joy in the Lord, you who are right with Him. . . .
For the Word of the Lord is right. He is faithful in
all He does. . . . Honor Him. For He spoke, and it
was done. He spoke with strong words, and it stood
strong. . . . The plans of the Lord stand forever. . . .
Happy are the people He has chosen for His own.
PSALM 33:1, 4, 8–9, 11–12 NLV

. . . .

Your Word is amazing, Father God. Your plans never fail. Your promises are sure and certain. You speak, and it is done. You said, "Let there be light," and there was light. Help me, Lord, to trust both You and Your Word. To do as You would have me do. Help me not to be discouraged when things don't go the way I planned. Remind me that *You* are the Master planner and that *I can trust* in Your plans. As I abide by Your Word, continually strengthened, guided, and empowered, I find the joy You have waiting for me. For I, Your chosen daughter, rest upon Your promises. Thank You, Father God. Amen.

Day 159

FOREVER PEACE

*The people who walked in darkness have seen a great
light; those who dwelt in a land of deep darkness, on them
has light shone. . . . For to us a child is born, to us a son
is given; and the government shall be upon his shoulder,
and his name shall be called Wonderful Counselor, Mighty
God, Everlasting Father, Prince of Peace. Of the increase
of his government and of peace there will be no end.*
ISAIAH 9:2, 6–7 ESV

. . . .

There are some days more than others, Lord, when I desperately need to find my way back into Your light. So I come to You today for that extra bit of "Son-shine" I need to lift myself up out of the darkness of this world and pull free from the shadows that try to drag me down, out, and away from You. So here I am, Lord, opening myself up to Christ. Allow Him to fill me with His wisdom, strength, and eternal power, and most of all His forever peace, unlimited and unending. In Jesus' name I pray, amen.

Day 160

A FAITHFUL SERVANT

*Master, you entrusted to me five talents; see, here
I have gained five talents more. His master said to
him, Well done, you upright (honorable, admirable)
and faithful servant! You have been faithful and
trustworthy over a little; I will put you in charge
of much. Enter into and share the joy (the delight,
the blessedness) which your master enjoys.*

MATTHEW 25:20–21 AMPC

. . . .

I want to be a good servant for You, Lord. I want to use
the things with which You have gifted me, not hide them.
So, dear Lord, give me the courage I need to step out for
You. Help me nurture the talents You've given me, then
use them for the good of others and for Your glory. Show
me what You would have me do, what You would want
me to use to benefit Your kingdom. Help me to be faithful
with what You have provided. I long for the day when we
meet face-to-face. The day when You open Your arms to
me and say, "Well done, My faithful daughter. Come to Me
and share the joy and blessings waiting for you." Amen.

Day 161

WHEN ALL'S RIGHT

Right will build a home in the fertile field. And where there's Right, there'll be Peace and the progeny of Right: quiet lives and endless trust. My people will live in a peaceful neighborhood—in safe houses, in quiet gardens. The forest of your pride will be clear-cut, the city showing off your power leveled. But you will enjoy a fortunate life, planting well-watered fields and gardens, with your farm animals grazing freely.

ISAIAH 32:16–20 MSG

. . . .

There are days, Lord, when I despair of finding the peace I crave within and without. And then I enter the land of Your words, which soothe my soul and buoy my spirit. For You speak of how, when all is right, we will find peace. And in that place of right and peace, I'll find the quiet life and endless trust I yearn for, surrounded by peace, safety, and calmness. Clear away my pride as if it were flammable brush. I know that I can only get to that place of peace with the help of Your words and Your powerful Spirit. Take me there now, Lord. Show me the freedom of a quiet life and endless trust. In Jesus' name, amen.

Day 162

A TIME FOR EVERYTHING

For everything there is a season, and a time for every matter under heaven: a time to be born, and a time to die; a time to plant, and a time to pluck up what is planted; a time to kill, and a time to heal; a time to break down, and a time to build up; a time to weep, and a time to laugh; a time to mourn, and a time to dance.
ECCLESIASTES 3:1–4 ESV

Your Word, Lord, tells me there's a time for everything that happens—life and death, planting and sowing, weeping and laughing, mourning and dancing. And that's just the beginning of Your list. But I get it, Lord. I know some days I'll be sick, praying for Your healing touch. Other days I may be mourning, seeking Your comfort. But through all these seasons, Lord, help me to maintain an undercurrent of Your joy, no matter what my day brings. Help me to realize that someday all these seasons will pass. In the meantime, I can develop into the woman You created me to be and then dip into Your stream of joy, because I have my hope in heaven with You. Amen.

Day 163

THE BUILD-UP

*Let us no longer criticize one another. Instead decide
never to put a stumbling block or pitfall in your brother's
way. . . . The kingdom of God is not eating and drinking,
but righteousness, peace, and joy in the Holy Spirit.
Whoever serves Christ in this way is acceptable to God
and approved by men. So then, we must pursue what
promotes peace and what builds up one another.*
ROMANS 14:13, 17–19 HCSB

I've seen the damage that divisive people can afflict on
others, Lord. Even worse, there may have been times when
I myself caused contention because I criticized someone.
Whether my criticism was to make myself feel superior or
to make another feel inferior doesn't seem to matter. For I
know You would have me encourage rather than discourage
the people in my life, whether they be strangers, relatives,
friends, or enemies. So, in my effort to pursue peace and
promote it, I'm determined to build others up and bring
Christ's light and love into their lives, allowing them to
see and experience a bit of God's kingdom. For it is there
that being right with God, the peace of Christ, and the joy
of the Spirit reign. Amen.

Day 164

HELP AND SHIELD

*No king is saved by the power of his strong army.
A soldier is not saved by great strength. A horse cannot
be trusted to win a battle. Its great strength cannot save
anyone. . . . Our soul waits for the Lord. He is our help
and our safe cover. For our heart is full of joy in Him,
because we trust in His holy name. O Lord, let Your
loving-kindness be upon us as we put our hope in You.*
PSALM 33:16–17, 20–22 NLV

Lord, sometimes I grow impatient. Instead of waiting for You to move, I find myself trusting in something other than You to save me. I begin to scheme, to make plans, to search for my own solutions. Yet those ideas never seem to work, and I just muck things up even more, within and without. I realize I cannot rely on anyone's strength but Yours, Lord. So please give me the gift of patience. Help me to wait on You, my help and shield, knowing that You've got everything under control. Your timing is the best. As I put my hope in You alone, my heart fills with joy. For You will work all things out for my good, here and beyond. Amen.

Day 165

PEACE-SPEAK

I will listen to what God the Lord will say. For He will speak peace to His people, to those who are right with Him. But do not let them turn again to foolish things. For sure His saving power is near those who fear Him, so His shining-greatness may live in the land. Loving-kindness and truth have met together. Peace and what is right and good have kissed each other.

PSALM 85:8–10 NLV

Since You entered my life, Lord, things have been different. I'm seeing things more clearly, hearing and understanding what You would have me do or not do. But what I seem to be needing more and more of is a sense of peace. Lord, I want to live a life where no matter what is happening within me or around me, I'm still residing beside Your still waters and lying down in Your green pastures. So give me this moment, Lord, in which I can catch my breath as I lean back against You. After I willingly offer up my problems to You, Lord, speak Your peace to me. In Jesus' name, amen.

Day 166

HIDDEN TREASURE

"God's kingdom is like a treasure hidden in a field for years and then accidentally found by a trespasser. The finder is ecstatic—what a find!—and proceeds to sell everything he owns to raise money and buy that field. Or, God's kingdom is like a jewel merchant on the hunt for exquisite pearls. Finding one that is flawless, he immediately sells everything and buys it."

MATTHEW 13:44–46 MSG

I know my only path to joy, Lord Jesus, is to sacrifice all that I am and have so that I can gain Your kingdom. Through You, I can reach out to Father God, tap into His power, gain His blessing, get the guidance I need to do as He bids, and so much more. So help me, Jesus, to put You above all things. To seek You before all else. To turn to You upon waking in the morning and then just before I turn out the light at night. For the only joy upon earth is to be focused upon You in heaven. To be in Your presence, feel Your embrace, and be showered by Your love and kindness. What a treasure! What a find! In Your name, I pray and rejoice. Amen.

Day 167

HOPE AND HARMONY

Whatever was written in the past was written for our instruction, so that we may have hope through endurance and through the encouragement from the Scriptures. Now may the God who gives endurance and encouragement allow you to live in harmony with one another, according to the command of Christ Jesus. . . . Now may the God of hope fill you with all joy and peace as you believe in Him so that you may overflow with hope by the power of the Holy Spirit.

ROMANS 15:4–5, 13 HCSB

. . . .

Your scriptures, Lord, are my gateway to You. Your stories help me understand who You are and how I can grow closer to You. Your testaments encourage me to learn more about who You are and how You see me. Your Psalms read like my journal, where a myriad of emotions and thoughts align so well with my own. Your Word makes me feel loved, whole, and full of hope. God of fortitude and confidence, help me find a way to live in peace with others, just as Christ commanded I do. Spirit of hope, fill me with Your joy and peace. Amen.

VALLEY OF BLESSING

Jehoshaphat and his people came to take away what they wanted. . .more than they could carry. It took them three days to take all the things, because there was so much. They gathered together in the Valley of Beracah [blessing] on the fourth day. There they praised and thanked the Lord. . . . They returned to Jerusalem with joy. For the Lord had filled them with joy by saving them.
2 CHRONICLES 20:25–27 NLV

. . . .

How wonderful to know, Lord, that when I'm in trouble and I lay my problem down before You, ask for Your advice, and vow to do as You say, You move into action. You turn what seem like impossible situations into amazing victories. You turn curses into blessings. When I pray, You do things beyond my imagining. For there is nothing You cannot do. No problem You cannot fix. No curse You cannot undo. And before I know it, I find myself in the Valley of Blessing. Thank You, Lord, for not just saving me but championing me. For not just answering one prayer but thousands. For working in my life and filling me with irrepressible joy in You. Amen.

Day 169

REKINDLE

Stir up (rekindle the embers of, fan the flame of, and keep burning) the [gracious] gift of God, [the inner fire] that is in you. . . . For God did not give us a spirit of timidity (of cowardice, of craven and cringing and fawning fear), but [He has given us a spirit] of power and of love and of calm and well-balanced mind and discipline and self-control.

2 TIMOTHY 1:6–7 AMPC

Too often, Lord, I feel like I'm not living my life from a place of courage. I allow my fears to rule me more than my faith. Help me, Lord, to turn things around. Give me a new outlook. Help me rekindle my passion to use the gifts You've given me—and to do so without fear of the views or opinions of others. I serve and worship You alone. For You alone fuel me with a spirit of power, love, peace, clear thinking, discipline, and control, enabling me to do so much more than I ever asked or even imagined. In Jesus' name, amen.

Day 170

SEEKING JESUS

*Mary Magdalene and the other Mary went to see
the tomb. . . . The angel said to the women, "Do not
be afraid, for I know that you seek Jesus. . . . He is
going before you to Galilee; there you will see him." . . .
They departed quickly from the tomb with fear
and great joy. . . . And behold, Jesus met them and
said, "Greetings!" And they. . .worshiped him.*
MATTHEW 28:1, 5, 7–9 ESV

Like the Marys, I too, Lord, am a female disciple. As such, I want to be as faithful to You as they were. Without fear, I look for You. With faith, I find You. And I'm never going to let You go. Be with me now. Help me look beyond myself and my assumptions and look to You and Your truth. I want to walk in Your will and way. To hear Your voice speak. To tell others where they can find You, what they can tell You, and how You will appear at the sound of our plea and prayer. Knowing that each day I can and will see You fills me with joy as I bow down at Your feet, ready to worship, to listen, to serve. In Your name, amen.

Day 171
SO MUCH

The Lord Who bought you and saves you, the Holy One of Israel, says, "I am the Lord your God, Who teaches you to do well, Who leads you in the way you should go. If only you had listened to My Laws! Then your peace would have been like a river and your right-standing with God would have been like the waves of the sea."
ISAIAH 48:17–18 NLV

. . . .

Ah Lord, there is so much I owe You, so much You've done for me that I can never repay. Yet there are some things I *can* do to honor You. I can abide by Your teachings, so please make Your lessons plain, Lord. I can follow Your leading, so open my eyes to Your signposts. And I can listen to Your Word, so open my ears so I can clearly hear You. Then I will have Your perpetual and constantly flowing peace. Then I will find Your blessings coming to me like waves rolling in from the sea. Ah Lord, there is so much I owe You, forever and ever. Amen.

MY GOD, MY HELP

O send out Your light and Your truth, let them lead me. . .to Your dwelling. Then will I go to the altar of God, to God, my exceeding joy. . . . Why are you cast down, O my inner self? And why should you. . . be disquieted within me? Hope in God and wait expectantly for Him, for I shall yet praise Him, Who is the help of my [sad] countenance, and my God.
PSALM 43:3–5 AMPC

Lord, I come to Your Word. Send Your light out to me. Allow it to reveal the truth You would have me know. Let the light of Your Word lead me into Your presence, the place where I find my peace, feel Your touch, and experience unfathomable joy. Calm my soul, Lord. Erase my anxiety. Be the balm to my inner self. Renew my hope, Lord. Help me to wait for You, to expect Your goodness to meet my prayer. Give me these moments of quiet. Make my spirit as calm as still water. And as I rest here with You, I give You all my praise and the joy that comes with it. Amen.

Day 173

IN GOOD HANDS

The fruit of the [Holy] Spirit [the work which His presence within accomplishes] is love, joy (gladness), peace, patience (an even temper, forbearance), kindness, goodness (benevolence), faithfulness, gentleness (meekness, humility), self-control (self-restraint, continence). . . If we live by the [Holy] Spirit, let us also walk by the Spirit. [If by the Holy Spirit we have our life in God, let us go forward walking in line, our conduct controlled by the Spirit.]
GALATIANS 5:22–23, 25 AMPC

Lord, You have created me, Your Son has saved me, and Your Spirit produces in me all the positive characteristics—love, joy, peace, patience, kindness, goodness, faithfulness, gentleness, self-control—of a godly daughter. Help me, Lord, to allow Your Spirit to work in me in every and any way He can. Make me look, speak, act, listen, and walk just as Jesus did. I wish to follow in His steps, even though at times I know that road may be rocky. Still, no matter the terrain, I know I am in good hands, moving forward, my steps solidly in line with Yours and my actions controlled by Your Spirit. Amen.

Day 174

A GREAT LIGHT

Gloom will not be upon her who is distressed. . . .
The people who walked in darkness have seen a great
light. . . . Upon them a light has shined. . . . They rejoice
before You. . . . For unto us a Child is born, unto us a
Son is given. . . . And His name will be called Wonderful,
Counselor, Mighty God, Everlasting Father, Prince of Peace.
ISAIAH 9:1–3, 6 NKJV

When the shadows of sadness come upon me, Lord, rise up. Shine Your light down on me. Break up the gloom that threatens to envelop me. Expel the darkness so that I may rejoice in Your "Son-shine." You are the wonder of my life. You have the guidance I need to walk Your way. Deliver me with Your mighty power. Counsel me with Your wisdom. Let no one snatch me out of Your hand. Be my forever Father, my shield, my protector, my Abba God. Be the priceless Prince with whom I live happily ever after in this world and the next. Lord, surround me with Your peace, love, grace, and mercy as I abide in You. In Jesus' name, amen.

Day 175

THE NEWS

"Seek the LORD while he may be found; call upon him while he is near; let the wicked forsake his way, and the unrighteous man his thoughts; let him return to the LORD. . . . For my thoughts are not your thoughts, neither are your ways my ways, declares the LORD. For as the heavens are higher than the earth, so are my ways higher than your ways and my thoughts than your thoughts."

ISAIAH 55:6–9 ESV

Lord, although I don't consider myself very wicked or unrighteous, I am having a difficult time with my mindset. I feel I'm being inundated with nothing but bad news. And that bad news affects my thoughts, leading me to despair, conflict, and hopelessness. So here I am, Lord, coming to You once more for some much-needed help. Give me the strength to memorize Your Word (aka thoughts) so that I can live my life more in line with how You would have me live it. Help me spend less time watching, reading, and listening to the world news and more time watching, reading, and listening to Your good news. In Jesus' name, amen.

Day 176

EYE-OPENER

They began to recognize God and praise and give thanks. . . . God has visited His people [in order to help and care for and provide for them]! And this report concerning [Jesus] spread. . . . In that very hour Jesus was healing many [people] of sicknesses and distressing bodily plagues and evil spirits, and to many who were blind He gave [a free, gracious, joy-giving gift of] sight.
LUKE 7:16–17, 21 AMPC

. . . .

I am still amazed, Father God, by the gift You have given me in Your Son, Jesus. Through Him, You came and walked among us. You are and have been my helper, caretaker, and provider. You heal me from the sickness within my body, mind, spirit, and soul. You de-stress me, taking away my cares, woes, anxieties, and issues. You have opened my eyes to the truth of Your Word. Through that lens, I see the path You want me to take, the road You want me to travel. Thank You for the joy-giving gift of Jesus, the one who continually opens my eyes, mind, and heart so that I can see You. In His name I pray, amen.

Day 177

THE POWER OF THE WORD

*"The rain and snow come down from heaven and do
not return there without giving water to the earth.
This makes plants grow on the earth, and gives seeds to
the planter and bread to the eater. So My Word which
goes from My mouth will not return to Me empty. It will
do what I want it to do, and will carry out My plan well.
You will go out with joy, and be led out in peace."*
ISAIAH 55:10–12 NLV

So much power resides within Your Word, Lord. Whatever
You say, whatever flows from Your mouth, in no way returns
to You empty. For Your Word does whatever You want it
to do. It carries out Your plans, ideas, and purpose. The
beauty and wonder of it is that Your Word holds so much
power for and within me—and it is there for me to tap
into anytime day or night. So, Lord, today, along with Your
blessing me with Your strength, bless me with Your peace
as I live within and by Your Word. In Jesus' name I pray,
amen.

Day 178

GOOD WORDS

Lying is in the heart of those who plan what is bad,
but those who plan peace have joy. . . . The Lord hates
lying lips, but those who speak the truth are His joy. . . .
Worry in the heart of a man weighs it down, but a good
word makes it glad. . . . Life is in the way of those who
are right with God, and in its path there is no death.

PROVERBS 12:20, 22, 25, 28 NLV

. . . .

You, Lord, are the Master of truth and the archenemy of the father of lies. So, Lord, help me be very aware of all the words I allow to leave my lips. Keep me on the path of truth so that I will be a person who makes plans for peace. For I want to please You and partake of all the joy that offers. I realize worries are nothing more than lies I tell myself. They imply that I don't trust You. So filter my words, Lord. Keep any and all untruths from my mind and lips because my desire is to be right with You in thought, word, and deed. Amen.

Day 179

THE IMPORTANT THING

I do not want to be proud of anything except in the cross of our Lord Jesus Christ. Because of the cross, the ways of this world are dead to me, and I am dead to them. If a person does or does not go through the religious act of becoming a Jew, it is worth nothing. The important thing is to become a new person. Those who follow this way will have God's peace and loving-kindness. They are the people of God.
GALATIANS 6:14–16 NLV

You have begun a new work in me, Lord. You, Your Son, and Your Spirit, as well as Your Word, have begun to transform me, to make me into a new woman—a woman of God. To get there from here, Lord, I need Your supernatural power and support, as well as some new strength every day. I need Your help as I learn to live and move in Your Spirit, to refresh, renew, and transform my mind, to sing this new song You have composed and planted in my heart. I thank You for giving me Your peace and loving-kindness as I follow this way. In Jesus' name, amen.

Day 180

GOOD NEWS

*There were shepherds in the fields. . .watching their flocks
of sheep at night. The angel of the Lord came to them.
The shining-greatness of the Lord shone around them.
They were very much afraid. The angel said to them,
"Do not be afraid. See! I bring you good news of
great joy which is for all people. Today, One Who
saves from the punishment of sin has been
born. . . . He is Christ the Lord."*

LUKE 2:8–11 NLV

. . . .

I love how You gave Your Son's birth announcement to
humankind, Lord. You directed angels to proclaim the
great news, the good news, about Jesus to a simple band
of shepherds, socially considered one of the lowest groups
of people. The angel's first words to them were, "Don't be
afraid. I've got some good news that's going to bring you
great happiness. Jesus, God's Son, will save you!" When *I*
first heard Your news, it seemed too good to be true—that
someone sacrificed all so that I could live for You, see You,
pray to You. Yet that good news was, still is, and forever
will be true. Thank You for the joy I find in Jesus, Your
Son and my Lord, King, and Savior. Amen.

PEACE LIKE A RIVER

*For thus says the Lord: Behold, I will extend peace
to her like a river, and the glory of the nations like
an overflowing stream; then you will be nursed,
you will be carried on her hip and trotted [lovingly
bounced up and down] on her [God's maternal]
knees. As one whom his mother comforts, so will I
comfort you; you shall be comforted in Jerusalem.*
ISAIAH 66:12–13 AMPC

Oh Lord, what I wouldn't do to have peace like a river
attending my way, helping me live a life for You in such
a chaotic world during such a chaotic time. Yet peace is
not just what You promised me but also what You left me
(John 14:27). You don't just give me peace; You care for me
as a mother cares for her darling child. You nourish me,
Abba, as no one else can. You allow me to cling to You as
You carry me on Your hip. You even lovingly bounce me
up and down on Your knee. Remind me of this promised
peace and Your attention to care, Lord, when anxiety comes
to call. Continue to comfort me as only You can. In Jesus'
name, amen.

Day 182

THE VOICE OF JOY

Show your happiness, all peoples! Call out to God with
the voice of joy! For the Lord Most High is to be feared.
He is a great King over all the earth. He sets people under
us, and nations under our feet. He chooses for us what
is to be ours, the pride of Jacob, whom He loves. . . .
God rules over the nations. God sits on His holy throne.
PSALM 47:1–4, 8 NLV

. . . .

It seems so easy, Lord, for me to get weighed down by
world news. I sometimes feel so helpless, unable to stop
the tide of evil. Yet that's not how You would have me be.
For I'm Your child. You're my King, the one who rules over
all things, who chooses what I am to be and have in this
life. You want me to be filled with joy. For what kind of
witness would I be for You if I were constantly worried,
frightened, upset, and anxious? So, Lord, today, right here,
right now, turn my frown upside down! Give me that deep
sense of joy from which I can draw—no matter what's
happening within and without. In Jesus' name I pray and
praise, amen.

Day 183

MY MAKER

*Fear not, for you shall not be ashamed; neither be
confounded and depressed, for you shall not be put to
shame. For you shall forget the shame of your youth,
and you shall not [seriously] remember the reproach of your
widowhood any more. For your Maker is your Husband—
the Lord of hosts is His name—and the Holy One of Israel
is your Redeemer; the God of the whole earth He is called.*

ISAIAH 54:4–5 AMPC

. . . .

Life can be lonely, Lord, whether a person is married, single,
or widowed. That's why I take such joy in looking to You
to fulfill me in every way. For You have claimed that You,
my Maker, are also my husband. You, the Lord of Hosts,
are my Redeemer. You, the God of the whole earth, are
also my Father, my beloved, my rock and refuge. Knowing
You are all things to me, from *A* to *Z*, I will not fear nor
be ashamed, confused, or depressed. Because You are my
all in all, there is nothing else and no one else I need to
feel complete, loved, and chosen. Thank You, my Savior,
for loving me so. In Jesus' name, amen.

Day 184

THE HABIT OF JOYFUL HOPE

*Let us. . .rejoice in our sufferings, knowing that
pressure and affliction and hardship produce patient
and unswerving endurance. And endurance (fortitude)
develops maturity of character (approved faith and tried
integrity). And character [of this sort] produces [the
habit of] joyful and confident hope of eternal salvation.
Such hope never disappoints or deludes or shames
us, for God's love has been poured out in our hearts
through the Holy Spirit Who has been given to us.*
ROMANS 5:3–5 AMPC

Even when I feel as if I'm going through the wringer, Lord,
I have hope. For Your Word tells me that my troubles are
actually good for me. They strengthen me. They bring me
back to You. They remind me of the joy I have because I
know I will one day be with You in heaven forever. And
it is that hope that keeps me going, looking to You, feeling
Your love bloom within me through the Holy Spirit You've
given me. Within You, Lord, I have all I need not just to get
through this life but to experience Your abundant peace
and provision amid the process. Amen.

Day 185

MOTHER WISDOM

Wisdom cries aloud in the street, she raises her voice in the markets. . . . If you will turn (repent) and give heed to my reproof, behold, I [Wisdom] will pour out my spirit upon you, I will make my words known to you. . . . Whoso hearkens to me [Wisdom] shall dwell securely and in confident trust and shall be quiet, without fear or dread of evil.
PROVERBS 1:20, 23, 33 AMPC

. . . .

Oh God of wisdom, I seek Your help and advice. Please answer my call. Pour out Your Spirit on me. Then, as You speak to my mind and heart, help me comprehend Your words. Answer my questions, make clear Your response, and give me tools to apply Your knowledge and understanding to my life. Help me not to be too sensitive when You scold me but to take Your advice and allow it to draw me ever closer to You. I ask all these things, knowing that the more I heed Your wisdom, the more secure I'll be and the more I'll live in peace with trust, confidence, and courage. Amen.

Day 186

A FOREVER GUIDE

*Fair and beautiful in elevation, is the joy of all
the earth—Mount Zion [the City of David]. . . .
God has made Himself known in her palaces as a
Refuge (a High Tower and a Stronghold). . . . We have
thought of Your steadfast love, O God, in the midst
of Your temple. . . . For this God is our God forever
and ever; He will be our guide [even] until death.*
PSALM 48:2–3, 9, 14 AMPC

. . . .

It's hard to imagine, Lord, that You chose me as Your vessel.
My fragile body is Your amazing temple. Therein You guide,
love, help, and strengthen me. You have made Yourself
known to me as a refuge. To You I run, knowing You will
shield me in Your high tower. You will defend me, for You
are my supernatural stronghold. And in the midst of all
this, I am overwhelmed by Your lavish love. You are mine
and I am Yours forever and ever. Continue, Lord, to fill
me with Your joy. Be my guide here and now, and even to
death and beyond. In Jesus' name I pray, amen.

A FOREVER KIND OF LOVE

"This exile is just like the days of Noah for me: I promised
then that the waters of Noah would never again flood
the earth. I'm promising now no more anger, no more
dressing you down. For even if the mountains walk away
and the hills fall to pieces, my love won't walk away
from you, my covenant commitment of peace won't fall
apart." The GOD who has compassion on you says so.
ISAIAH 54:9–10 MSG

How soothing, how wonderful, how lovely to know, Lord,
that You have promised me a forever kind of love. Even
if mountains are leveled and hills fall into the sea, You
will continue to love me. No matter what happens, Your
covenant of peace will neither be shaken nor fall apart.
Your love for me, for *all* Your daughters, is more than I
can take in, Lord. There are very few things in my life
that are certain, but You, Lord, are one of them. Thank
You for loving me through the rough patches, for sticking
with me when all others deserted me. My love won't walk
away from You. Amen.

Day 188

OCCUPIED WITH JOY

What I have seen to be good and fitting is to eat and drink and find enjoyment in all the toil with which one toils under the sun the few days of his life that God has given him, for this is his lot. Everyone also to whom God has given wealth and possessions and power to enjoy them, and to accept his lot and rejoice in his toil—this is the gift of God. For he will not much remember the days of his life because God keeps him occupied with joy in his heart.

ECCLESIASTES 5:18–20 ESV

This is what I want, Lord. To enjoy the life You have given me. To enjoy whatever I eat and drink and whatever work I put my hand to. For this is the life with which You have so wonderfully blessed me. I want to be so focused on all the good things in my life, so content with what You have gifted me that I don't get hung up on the negative things. I don't want to allow the world's woes to put a shadow upon my blessings from You. Keep me occupied, Lord, with all the joy You have already planted in my heart, today and every day. Amen.

Day 189

LOVING

Jesus said to him, " 'You must love the Lord your God with all your heart and with all your soul and with all your mind.' This is the first and greatest of the Laws. The second is like it, 'You must love your neighbor as you love yourself.' All the Laws and the writings of the early preachers depend on these two most important Laws."
MATTHEW 22:37–40 NLV

. . . .

Today, Lord, I pray for the people of the world to heed Jesus' greatest commandments: to love You with all their heart, soul, and mind; and to love their neighbors as they love themselves. For, Lord, if everyone in the world loved You above all things and others as well as themselves, there would be no wars or crimes. People would be looking out for each other, helping each other, taking care of each other—and loving You. Along with praying for others to love, I ask You, Lord, to help me to love others—beginning with You. To do so gladly and with my entire being. Help me to love myself, which can be difficult at times, so that I can learn how to love others. In Jesus' name, amen.

Day 190

THE AGENDA FOR REJOICING

*Jesus said. . ."See what I've given you? Safe passage
as you walk on snakes and scorpions, and protection
from every assault of the Enemy. No one can put a hand
on you. All the same, the great triumph is not in your
authority over evil, but in God's authority over you and
presence with you. Not what you do for God but what
God does for you—that's the agenda for rejoicing."*
LUKE 10:19–20 MSG

You have provided me with so many blessings, Jesus, it's hard to count them all. You give me safe passage through this life. Because I live in You, nothing can ever really touch me. No power can ever get through because You're busy protecting me. In fact, no one can even take me out of Your hand! But that's not where my real triumph is. My real triumph is Abba God's power over me and His presence within me. It's not about what I do for God, how He works through me. No. My real cause for rejoicing is all about what He does for me! Thank You, Jesus, for all the blessings You so readily give me and all the ways You work in my life. Amen.

BLINDINGLY OBVIOUS

Be cheerful. Keep things in good repair. Keep your spirits up. Think in harmony. Be agreeable. Do all that, and the God of love and peace will be with you for sure. Greet one another with a holy embrace. All the brothers and sisters here say hello. The amazing grace of the Master, Jesus Christ, the extravagant love of God, the intimate friendship of the Holy Spirit, be with all of you.
2 CORINTHIANS 13:11–14 MSG

. . . .

Lord, I want to do what You would have me do, to follow Your lead in all things. Yet oftentimes, I am going to need Your help, because some things don't come to me as naturally as they do for others. So as I walk this road with You, Lord, help me to have an optimistic outlook. To see and focus on the good in all things and people, even if the not so good is blindingly obvious. Help me encourage others, including myself, by planting good words and seeds of love in their midst. Give me a mind that thinks with compassion, not conflict. And as I do these things, Lord, may it be blindingly obvious to others that You, the God of peace and love, are with me. Amen.

Day 192

OPEN MINDS

At that, Jesus rejoiced, exuberant in the Holy Spirit.
"I thank you, Father, Master of heaven and earth, that you
hid these things from the know-it-alls and showed them
to these innocent newcomers. Yes, Father, it pleased
you to do it this way." . . . He then turned in a private
aside to his disciples. "Fortunate the eyes that see what
you're seeing. . .to hear what you are hearing."
LUKE 10:21, 23 MSG

Your Word is so precious to me, Lord. The fact that I can pick up my Bible and read about You is amazing. I too was once a vast wasteland. And then You and Your Word hovered over me. You said, "Let there be light," and I saw the truth for the first time. I heard Your voice speak deep into my spirit. Help me never take for granted the fact that, through Your Word, I can see how You have been moving. Thank You for letting me read, see, and hear Your story from Genesis to Revelation—for opening my simple mind to the power of Your Word. Every page I turn, every passage I read, prompts me to rejoice in spirit, soul, mind, and heart. Amen.

WITHIN YOUR WALLS

I was glad when they said to me, "Let us go to the house of the Lord." . . . May all go well for those who love you. May there be peace within your walls. May all go well within your houses. I will now say, "May peace be within you," for the good of my brothers and my friends. Because of the house of the Lord our God, I will pray for your good.
PSALM 122:1, 6–9 NLV

. . . .

Something happens to me, Lord, when I come into Your house, when I step into Your sanctuary, Your place of peace. That's when I am most conscious of Your world totally surrounding me—my walls within Yours and Your walls within mine. Me in You and You in me is a safe place to be in a world often fraught with conflict. Help me, Lord, to carry that sense of place and peace within myself so that wherever I am, my connection to You is firm and sure. And as I appropriate Your peace, Lord, and make it my own, give me the opportunity to share it with others. To bless them with peace within their walls, houses, and deep within. May Your peace reign. Amen.

Day 194

LOST AND FOUND

"What woman, having ten silver coins, if she loses one coin, does not light a lamp, sweep the house, and search carefully until she finds it? And when she has found it, she calls her friends and neighbors together, saying, 'Rejoice with me, for I have found the piece which I lost!' Likewise, I say to you, there is joy in the presence of the angels of God over one sinner who repents."

LUKE 15:8–10 NKJV

. . . .

Lord, through Your Word I realize I can, with Your help, bring joy not only to others but to You and Your angels. I know there are many people out there, many sheep who have yet to find You, the Good Shepherd. Yet I also know that You can use me to find them—to be the light that attracts them to You. So help me, Lord, to be that light—to allow Your love and joy to shine through me so powerfully that others will want what I have: You. To that end, I pray, Lord, that Your Holy Spirit would lead the way. That He would use me to turn nonbelievers to You. And that Your angels would then share in the joy of a lost sheep that has been found. In Jesus' name, amen.

Day 195

UNDISTURBED

May grace (God's unmerited favor) and spiritual peace [which means peace with God and harmony, unity, and undisturbedness] be yours from God our Father and from the Lord Jesus Christ. . . . You who once were [so] far away, through (by, in) the blood of Christ have been brought near. For He is [Himself] our peace (our bond of unity and harmony).
EPHESIANS 1:2; 2:13–14 AMPC

. . . .

Grace, favor, peace, harmony, unity, undisturbedness, brought near—the beauty of these words, Lord, leaves me breathless. Today, these words seem rarely used, for they are not reflective of the atmosphere in which we now live. And that is why I seek You, why I love delving into Your Word, why I continually plant Your good news within my heart. Today, Lord, pour down upon me, refresh me with Your grace and peace. Draw me ever closer so that I may feel Your presence and take in Your energy, life, and light. You—God, Jesus, Spirit—are my peace, my path, my passion, my provision. Keep me by Your side, undisturbed by the woes of the world, knowing You alone are my world. In Jesus' name I pray, amen.

Day 196

A QUENCHED THIRST

O God, You are my God. I will look for You with
all my heart and strength. My soul is thirsty for You.
My flesh is weak wanting You in a dry and tired land
where there is no water. . . . I have seen Your power
and Your shining-greatness. . . . I will lift up my
hands in Your name. My soul will be filled. . . .
And my mouth praises You with lips of joy.

PSALM 63:1–2, 4–5 NLV

Oh Lord, my God, I need You. I need Your presence, Your cooling shade, Your warming arms. You are everything I desire and thirst for. I am desperate for Your comfort and love. Give me some good news through Your Word. Show me Your power and might. Fill me with Your love and grace. Draw me out of myself and into Your presence. For here alone do I find my source, my provision, my strength, my refuge. In You, I am home. In You, I have hope. I'm lifting up my hands, Lord, to praise and worship You. Fill my soul with Your Spirit. My mouth will respond with praises of joy. In Jesus' name, amen.

SILENCE BEFORE GOD

*"'I'll be right there with [Jerusalem]'—GOD's Decree—
'a wall of fire around unwalled Jerusalem and a radiant
presence within.'" . . . Quiet, everyone! Shh! Silence before
GOD. Something's afoot in his holy house. He's on the
move! . . . When the Lamb ripped off the seventh seal,
Heaven fell quiet—complete silence for about half an hour.*
ZECHARIAH 2:4–5, 13; REVELATION 8:1 MSG

. . . .

In this ever-restless world, Lord, finding a place of quiet
is difficult. People are more apt to talk than listen. Or else
they escape the world's silence by filling their emptiness
with mindless games, social media, texts, emails, and the
like. It's all still noise, all still a distraction. Yet my path to
You, Lord, is paved with silence. For it's only when I truly
empty my mind and heart of all but You that I find my
place before You, beside You, sharing my thoughts, dreams,
ideas—and life. Thank You, Lord, for taking the time to sit
still with me, to rest, to find true and holy peace of mind,
heart, spirit, and soul. Come, greet me, Lord, as I enter into
Your silence, Your presence, Your love. Amen.

MOVED WITH COMPASSION

*When he came to himself, he said. . .I will get up
and go to my father, and I will say to him, Father,
I have sinned. . . . While he was still a long way off,
his father saw him and was moved with pity and
tenderness [for him]; and he ran and embraced him
and kissed him [fervently]. . . . The father said. . .
Let us revel and feast and be happy and make merry.*
LUKE 15:17–18, 20, 22–23 AMPC

. . . .

Sometimes, Lord, I don't realize how far I have strayed
from You. But then, when I come to myself, I know what
I have to say. I have to tell You, in my own words, how I
have erred and made a misstep. Help me right here and
now ask for Your forgiveness. Help me to picture You as a
Father who is looking for me, waiting for me, even when
I'm still a long way off. Let me see You as a Father who is
moved with love and compassion for me. Open Your arms,
Lord, as I turn this corner and run into Your embrace.
Grant me Your forgiveness. And may we end this moment
by reveling in each other's company, full of joy and feasting
on our mutual love. Amen.

Day 199

IN THE UNSEEN

You have seen my affliction, You have taken note of my
life's distresses, and. . .You have set my feet in a broad
place. . . . Oh, how great is Your goodness, which You
have laid up for those who fear, revere, and worship
You, goodness which You have wrought for those who
trust and take refuge in You before the sons of men!
In the secret place of Your presence You hide them.
PSALM 31:7–8, 19–20 AMPC

. . . .

When I'm tired, when I'm fraught with worries, when I'm desperate for some peace and one-on-one time with You, I find my way to that secret place I share with You alone. You, Lord, have seen the challenges I face, the opportunities they bring. You alone know everything I've ever done, thought, and said. You know me inside and out—and still You love me. Still You rescue me, giving me the guidance and direction I need to find my way. So here I am once more, Lord, coming to You, finding You in that special secret place in the unseen where peace, love, light, and You are found. Ah, that's better. Amen.

Day 200

AT HOME IN GOD

Silence is praise to you, Zion-dwelling God, and also obedience. You hear the prayer in it all. We all arrive at your doorstep sooner or later, loaded with guilt, our sins too much for us—but you get rid of them once and for all. Blessed are the chosen! Blessed the guest at home in your place! We expect our fill of good things in your house, your heavenly manse. . . . Dawn and dusk take turns calling, "Come and worship."

PSALM 65:1–4, 8 MSG

. . . .

In the stillness of this moment, Lord, I come before You, in silent wonder of who You are, what You have done, and how You have worked in my life. Hear my prayer, Lord, as my lips praise You. Free me of the missteps, the mistakes I have made, the guilt that weighs me down. Lord, cleanse me of all shadows. Leave only Your light behind and within me. Here, in Your presence, I feel I am home. Thank You for opening Your door to me. For choosing me, saving me, and loving me. What joy I find within these cloud-formed walls in Your heavenly dwelling, my provider, my God. Here I find all I need. Here, at Your feet, I worship. In Jesus' name, amen.

THE SEARCH

*I know the thoughts and plans that I have for you,
says the Lord, thoughts and plans for welfare and peace
and not for evil, to give you hope in your final outcome.
Then you will call upon Me, and you will come and pray
to Me, and I will hear and heed you. Then you will seek
Me, inquire for, and require Me [as a vital necessity] and
find Me when you search for Me with all your heart.*
JEREMIAH 29:11–13 AMPC

Lord, I know You have plans for me. Yet I feel I'm not
where I thought I'd be at this point in my life. I expected
something different, perhaps something better. And I'm a
bit concerned over what lies ahead. So help me, Lord, to
trust You with my future. For I know You have thought and
planned for me since before I was a twinkle in my father's
eye or a smile on my mother's lips. You have prepared a
good outcome for me, for peace in my life and not evil,
all so that I will have hope in my future. Open my ears to
Your Word; open my soul to Your love; open my spirit to
Your peace as I search for You with all of my heart. Amen.

Day 202

SEEKERS

*Zacchaeus. . .was a chief tax collector and was rich.
And he was seeking to see who Jesus was, but on account
of the crowd he could not. . . . So he ran on ahead and
climbed up into a sycamore tree to see him. . . . When Jesus
came to the place, he looked up and said to him, "Zacchaeus,
hurry and come down, for I must stay at your house today."
So he hurried and came down and received him joyfully.*
LUKE 19:2–6 ESV

Rich or poor, large or small, Lord, may I always run to catch sight of You. May I not let crowds or distance dissuade me from finding You. You, Lord Jesus, know all who seek Your face. You know our names, stories, and conditions. And still You call us to Yourself, telling us to speedily welcome You into our homes, our hearts. And all who do, all who truly want to see Your face, just as they are, Lord, those are the ones with whom You spend time. Those are the ones You save. Those are the ones who revel in the joy of Your presence. Speak to me, Lord. Just as I am. In You I pray, amen.

Day 203

STANDING STRONG

Take all the help you can get, every weapon God has issued, so that when it's all over but the shouting you'll still be on your feet. Truth, righteousness, peace, faith, and salvation are more than words. Learn how to apply them. You'll need them throughout your life. God's Word is an indispensable weapon. In the same way, prayer is essential in this ongoing warfare. Pray hard and long.
EPHESIANS 6:13–18 MSG

. . . .

I live in a topsy-turvy world, Lord. And I need all the help I can get. That's where You come in. Give me all the tools I need to be able to stand strong when challenges come my way. For with Your help, those challenges can be turned into opportunities for You to work through me in the world. Teach me, Lord, how to apply truth, right standing, peace, faith, and salvation to my life. Help me plant Your Word in my heart so that I'll have its support when the going gets tough. And most of all, Lord, help me then go deeper with prayer, the next greatest weapon available. What a comfort knowing You have provided me with all I need to be the woman You created me to be in this world and the next. Amen.

Day 204

WHITER THAN SNOW

O God, favor me because of Your loving-kindness.
Take away my wrong-doing because of the greatness
of Your loving-pity. . . . I have sinned against You,
and You only. . . . Take away my sin, and I will be clean.
Wash me, and I will be whiter than snow. Make me hear
joy and happiness. . . . Make a clean heart in me, O God.
PSALM 51:1, 4, 7–8, 10 NLV

. . . .

Lord, I have hurt someone. I have injured another person, and I'm filled with remorse. For not only have I harmed another, but I have disobeyed You in the process. Thus I have sinned against You at the same time. Both bring me shame, Lord. But doing wrong to You truly hurts my heart. So I come to You upon my knees. I ask You for forgiveness. For cleansing. For a new heart and a fresh start. Wash me within and without, Lord. Supply me with the words of apology to the person I have harmed. At the same time, Lord, help me forgive those who have hurt me. And before I leave this prayer, this place, this space, Lord, "make me hear joy and happiness" in You once more. Amen.

Day 205

BLESSED QUIET
FOR YOUR SOUL

*Come to Me, all you who labor and are heavy-
laden and overburdened, and I will cause you to
rest. [I will ease and relieve and refresh your souls.]
Take My yoke upon you and learn of Me, for I am
gentle (meek) and humble (lowly) in heart, and you
will find rest (relief and ease and refreshment and
recreation and blessed quiet) for your souls.*
MATTHEW 11:28–29 AMPC

Lord, I come to You in this moment, my back aching from
the load I've been carrying. It's too much for me to bear.
So I leave it at Your feet. Please, Jesus, give me the relief
I so desperately need. Help me recover my life, my heart,
my soul from the pressures of this world. Lead me to Your
kingdom so that I can find the relief and ease I need. Show
me, Lord, how to take a real break, a real rest. Help me
get back into Your rhythm, to walk in step with You, to
take a deep breath and relax, and to allow You to replace
my problems with Your peace. Bless my soul, Jesus, with
Your quiet. Amen.

Day 206
GRAND OPENINGS

They said to Him, "Stay with us". . . . As [Jesus] sat at the table with them, He took the bread and gave thanks and broke it. Then He gave it to them. And their eyes were opened and they knew Him. Then He left them and could not be seen. They said to each other, "Were not our hearts filled with joy when He talked to us on the road about what the Holy Writings said?"

LUKE 24:29–32 NLV

. . . .

As I walk upon the road of life, Lord, thinking about what I've seen and heard, walk with me. Stay with me. Reveal to me the meaning of Your Word. Open up my mind as I read Your scriptures. Open my eyes so that I can see You in all things, all events, from Genesis to Revelation and beyond. Feed me the bread of Your Word. Break it open for me so that its wisdom can pour out. Talk to me through every letter, line, verse, and chapter. Fill my heart with the joy of Your Word as we walk and talk on this road and beyond. In Your name, I pray, live, move, and have my being. Amen.

THE LINK TO ALL GOOD

*Praise the Lord, O my soul. And all that is
within me, praise His holy name. Praise the Lord,
O my soul. And forget none of His acts of kindness.
He forgives all my sins. He heals all my diseases.
He saves my life from the grave. He crowns me with
loving-kindness and pity. He fills my years with good
things and I am made young again like the eagle.*
PSALM 103:1–5 NLV

. . . .

When panic or problems threaten to steal my joy and peace
in You, Lord, You bring to mind all the things for which I
can praise You. And as I begin to think back to how much
You've done for me and with me, as my mind fills with all
the blessings—past and present, earthly and heavenly—I
have in You, my panic melts away and my problems dissi-
pate. So I thank You, Lord, for Your kindness, forgiveness,
healing power, and compassion. Thank You for filling my
years here on this earth with so many good things. But
most of all, thank You, Lord, for being my link to all that
is good, loving, peaceful, and eternal. Amen.

Day 208

NIGHT HOURS

My lips will praise You because Your loving-kindness is better than life. . . . On my bed I remember You. I think of You through the hours of the night. For You have been my help. And I sing for joy in the shadow of Your wings. My soul holds on to You. Your right hand holds me up. . . . All who are faithful to God will be full of joy.

PSALM 63:3, 6–8, 11 NLV

. . . .

Lord, there is no better or greater thing in my life than Your love for me and Your never-ending kindness to me. When I climb into bed at the end of the day, I think of You. I pray to You. I ask You for blessings, for compassion on me and those I love. And amid that nightly prayer to You, I not only fall asleep but into Your arms. Thank You for holding me, helping me, hiding me, and hovering over me. In You I find my rest, my shelter, my peace. I'm clinging to You, Lord, holding on tight. For You are my salvation. You are my joy. In You alone do I trust and find my way. Amen.

Day 209

LOOKING UP

*If then you have been raised with Christ [to a new life,
thus sharing His resurrection from the dead], aim at
and seek the [rich, eternal treasures] that are above,
where Christ is, seated at the right hand of God.
And set your minds and keep them set on what is above
(the higher things), not on the things that are on the earth.
For [as far as this world is concerned] you have died,
and your [new, real] life is hidden with Christ in God.*
COLOSSIANS 3:1–3 AMPC

. . . .

I'm losing my peace, Lord, and I think it's because my
eyes are in the wrong place. It seems I've been focusing
on everything *except* for You. So help me raise my sights,
Lord. Lift my head so I can seek the things that are above
this earth, the forever riches I have in knowing You and
Your Son. Lift my eyes and mind, Lord, so that I may see
the higher things, such as peace, love, understanding, compassion, empathy, and wisdom. Each day, lift my thoughts
ever higher. Transform my mind, shape my thoughts, so
that each day I may become more like Jesus, my hero,
Savior, and Prince of Peace. In His name I pray, amen.

Day 210

WONDER AND JOY

"Why are you troubled, and why do doubts arise in your hearts? See my hands and my feet, that it is I myself. Touch me, and see. For a spirit does not have flesh and bones as you see that I have." And when he had said this, he showed them his hands and his feet. And while they still disbelieved for joy and were marveling, he said to them, "Have you anything here to eat?"

LUKE 24:38–41 ESV

You amaze me, Lord. You show up out of nowhere whenever I need You. You tell me to calm down. Not to worry. Not to allow thoughts of doubt into my heart or mind. You point me to You, revealing all that You are and ever have been. You tell me the truth. That You are the Son of God, the one who died to save my soul. The one raised from the dead who lives to bring me to Father God. Some days, Lord, I cannot believe what You have done for me. I sit back amazed yet full of joy. Then You help me get on with the needs of the day, continually providing for me, leading me, guiding me. Oh Lord, You are my wonder and joy. Amen.

Day 211

TURN THINGS AROUND

"I will turn things around for the people. I'll give them a language undistorted, unpolluted, words to address God in worship and, united, to serve me with their shoulders to the wheel. . . . I'll leave a core of people among you who are poor in spirit. . . . They'll make their home in God. This core holy people will not do wrong. . . . Content with who they are and where they are, unanxious, they'll live at peace."
ZEPHANIAH 3:9, 12–13 MSG

. . . .

Lord, what peace I would have within myself if I could just be content with who I am and where I am. I keep comparing myself to other people, people who seem to have a better life. Yet those same people are as transient as I am. You have said, Lord, that Your people are foreigners here. We are strangers on this earth, for this is not our true home. So help me, Lord, to take my eyes off myself and focus them on You. Show me ways to make my home in You, content to be who You made me and to be where You have placed me. Free, easy, and at peace in You. Amen.

Day 212

A WILLING SPIRIT

*Make a clean heart in me, O God. Give me a new spirit
that will not be moved. Do not throw me away from
where You are. And do not take Your Holy Spirit from
me. Let the joy of Your saving power return to me.
And give me a willing spirit to obey you. . . . Then my
tongue will sing with joy about how right and good You are.*

PSALM 51:10–12, 14 NLV

I've fallen short, Lord. I've misstepped. And so here I
am before You, asking for forgiveness. For my sins to
be washed away. For a clean heart—and a new spirit. A
spirit that will be stronger, not so easily led into sin, not
so easily lured into temptation. Draw me near to You,
Lord. I want to snuggle up close, to feel Your breath, to
join my spirit with Yours. Return to me the joy of Your
saving power. And make my spirit willingly obey You.
For I know my true joy and path lie in Your way, not my
own. Set me straight, Lord. Prepare me and my path as
I joyfully praise You. Amen.

VIBRANT HARMONIES

*From beginning to end he's there, towering far above
everything, everyone. So spacious is he, so expansive,
that everything of God finds its proper place in him
without crowding. Not only that, but all the broken
and dislocated pieces of the universe—people and
things, animals and atoms—get properly fixed and
fit together in vibrant harmonies, all because of his
death, his blood that poured down from the cross.*
Colossians 1:18–20 MSG

Jesus, my Lord and Savior, when I think of all You went
through to save someone like me, I am very humbled and
grateful. For it was through Your innocent blood shed
on the cross that our Father made His peace with us. All
the broken bits, all the loose ends, all the creatures and
creations in the universe were made whole and complete
once more through You. Because of You, everything has
now been repaired, remade, renewed, and refreshed. All
is in harmony because of Your death. Yet because You
still live, because I still have access to You, I also have
access to Your peace. Help me, Lord, to live a life in tune
with You. Amen.

Day 214

OPEN TO UNDERSTANDING

He went on to open their understanding of the Word of God, showing them how to read their Bibles. . . . He then led them out of the city over to Bethany. Raising his hands he blessed them, and while blessing them, made his exit, being carried up to heaven. And they were on their knees, worshiping him. They returned to Jerusalem bursting with joy. They spent all their time in the Temple praising God.
LUKE 24:45, 50–52 MSG

I need Your help, Lord. I need You to open my mind, heart, and eyes as I read the Word. I want to understand what You're writing, saying, teaching. I want to love what You want me to love. I want to see the words You want me to see. I want to think the thoughts You want me to think. So lead me, Lord. Bless me as I lift my hands in praise and fall on my knees in worship. Give me such a good understanding of You and Your ways that I may return to and approach this earthly world, bursting with joy as I praise and pray in Your name. Amen.

THE HEAD-LIFTING GOD

*We couldn't settle down. The fights in the church
and the fears in our hearts kept us on pins and
needles. We couldn't relax because we didn't know
how it would turn out. Then the God who lifts up the
downcast lifted our heads and our hearts with the
arrival of Titus. We were glad just to see him, but the
true reassurance came in. . .how much you cared,
how much you grieved, how concerned you were for
me. I went from worry to tranquility in no time!*
2 CORINTHIANS 7:5–7 MSG

So often battles are going on outside me while at the same
time I'm fending off fears within me, Lord. Being so con-
flicted within and without makes it hard to be able to relax.
And constantly worrying about how things will turn out in
the end doesn't do much for my peace of mind and heart.
But then You send someone or something my way—an
encourager or a blessing—and suddenly, I'm looking up
once more. I'm remembering how much You care for me.
And before I know it, frets fly out the window and peace
stills my soul. Thank You, Lord, for being the lifter of my
head and my heart. Amen.

Day 216

THE BOUNTIFUL EARTH

You visit the earth and water it; you greatly enrich it;
the river of God is full of water; you provide their grain. . . .
You water its furrows abundantly, settling its ridges,
softening it with showers, and blessing its growth.
You crown the year with your bounty. . . . The pastures of the
wilderness overflow, the hills gird themselves with joy,
the meadows clothe themselves with flocks, the valleys deck
themselves with grain, they shout and sing together for joy.
PSALM 65:9–13 ESV

I thank You, Lord, for the gift of this earth. For Your tender care of it and Your never-ending love for it. Give me that same love of the earth, Lord. Help me to be a better care-taker, to do what You would have me do to keep its waters flowing. . .its animals bountiful. . .its hills, plains, and meadows alive, joyful, and productive. You are not just the God of creation but also the Lord of abundance. As You provide for the earth, the earth, in turn, provides for me and mine. Help me to remember that, Lord. To thank You for this good earth that sings joyfully together with me in praise of You. Amen.

SWEET SLEEP

Keep sound and godly Wisdom and discretion,
and they will be life to your inner self, and a gracious
ornament to your neck (your outer self). Then you
will walk in your way securely and in confident
trust, and you shall not dash your foot or stumble.
When you lie down, you shall not be afraid; yes,
you shall lie down, and your sleep shall be sweet.
PROVERBS 3:21–24 AMPC

. . . .

My day usually begins well, Lord, because I wake up with You in my mind and heart. But then, as my day goes on, I get distracted by the world. Before I know it, I'm doing, working, living, loving in *my* wisdom and strength, not Yours. That's when things start to fall apart. That's when I start to trip over my own thoughts and end up flat on my face. By the end of the day, I'm beaten and bruised and sleep becomes elusive at best. So help me regain my peace by keeping and following Your wisdom and ways all through my day. As I do, I know I'll find calm and sweet sleep in the secret place of Your presence. In Jesus' name, amen.

Day 218

GENUINE JOY

*Unlike the culture around you, always dragging you
down to its level of immaturity, God brings the best
out of you, develops well-formed maturity in you. . . .
If you're called to give aid to people in distress, keep
your eyes open and be quick to respond; if you work with
the disadvantaged, don't let yourself get irritated with
them or depressed by them. Keep a smile on your face.
Love from the center of who you are; don't fake it.*

ROMANS 12:2, 8–9 MSG

· ·

Help me, Lord Jesus, to be different from the culture around
me. Lift me up to You, lest I be dragged down into the
chaos of this world. Bring out the best in me so that I can
be a useful part of Your body. Open my eyes to people
whom You want me to help. Give me the resources to lift
them as You have lifted me. Keep me from getting irritated
by those who are weak, suffering, disadvantaged, poor,
or depressed. Help me to keep my mind, heart, and ears
open. Make me a good listener, free of judgment. And
above all, give me such deep joy that no matter who I am
helping, my smile toward them is genuine, an offshoot of
my happiness in and with You. Amen.

SIT BACK AND RELAX

Ruth told her everything that the man had done for her, adding, "And he gave me all this barley besides—six quarts! He told me, 'You can't go back empty-handed to your mother-in-law!'" Naomi said, "Sit back and relax, my dear daughter, until we find out how things turn out; this man isn't going to waste any time. Mark my words, he's going to get everything wrapped up today."

RUTH 3:16–18 MSG

. . . .

When I'm waiting to see how things are going to turn out, Lord, I don't just get anxious; I also get grouchy. Then, before I know it, all kinds of scenarios begin playing out in my mind. And soon, any semblance of peace that remained within me has taken flight. So help me take the advice that Naomi gave to Ruth, Lord. Help me not to worry or freak out over imaginary scenarios that may never come to pass, and instead "sit back and relax" until I see how things are going to turn out. Help me to leave all in Your hands, knowing You always know best. In Jesus' name, amen.

PRESENT JOY

*[The once-exiled and now returned Israelites] sang,
praising and giving thanks to the Lord, saying,
"For He is good, for His loving-kindness is upon Israel
forever." All the people called out with a loud voice
when they praised the Lord because the work on the
house of the Lord had begun. But many. . .had seen
the first house of the Lord. And they cried with a loud
voice. . . . But many called out for joy in a loud voice.*
EZRA 3:11–12 NLV

Sometimes, Lord, I can really mess up a good thing. Then when I try to rebuild, the new doesn't seem like it will be better than—or even as good as—what was there before. Either way, Lord, help me to have hope. To rejoice at whatever new thing You are doing. Although it may be okay to spend a little time grieving over the loss of what once was, don't let me stay there. Give me the courage to look away from the past and into the present. Help me to praise what You are doing now. To see the new thing You have prepared. To remember how good You have been, are now, and always will be. Enfold me in Your present joy. In Jesus' name, amen.

Day 221

RIGHT WITH GOD

"Do not worry. Do not keep saying, 'What will we eat?' or, 'What will we drink?' or, 'What will we wear?' The people who do not know God are looking for all these things. Your Father in heaven knows you need all these things. First of all, look for the holy nation of God. Be right with Him. All these other things will be given to you also."
MATTHEW 6:31–33 NLV

. . . .

One of my major challenges in life, Lord, is not worrying about anything and everything but leaving all my concerns and questions in Your hands. For that's the only way I'll be able to maintain the amazing peace I found in You when I first believed. Help me to remember that You, Lord, know everything I need in this world and beyond. In fact, You know—and have already waiting in the wings—all those things I'm going to need before they've even entered into my head. So, Lord, from now on, to maintain my peace, my first priority is to be right with You. My second is to trust that whatever I do need is already on its way. Amen.

Day 222

THE TRUE SOURCE

"You heard the words that I said, 'I am not the Christ,
but I have been sent before Him.' The man who has
just been married has the bride. The friend of the
man just married stands at his side and listens to
him. He has joy when he hears the voice of the man
just married. I am full of this joy. He must become
more important. I must become less important."
JOHN 3:28–30 NLV

Jesus, nothing gives me more joy than when I bring You to the attention of a nonbeliever—and then that nonbeliever begins to experience You, follow You, love and worship You as I do. But afterward, Lord, help me to slip away to the sidelines. To get out of the way of Your light. Help me to be humble enough to let the newly born in You know *You* are the source of both our joy. That You are the true path, the real way, and I am just a signpost along the road. For You alone are the one and only Son. The one who plants and nourishes the joy in our lives and love in our hearts. In Your name I pray, amen.

STEPPING OUT

*Peter, suddenly bold, said, "Master, if it's really you,
call me to come to you on the water." He said, "Come
ahead." Jumping out of the boat, Peter walked on
the water to Jesus. But when he looked down at the
waves churning beneath his feet, he lost his nerve
and started to sink. He cried, "Master, save me!"*
MATTHEW 14:28–30 MSG

. . . .

There are moments, Jesus, when I have courage and am
more than ready for the challenges before me. So I take a
bold step forward, knowing that You, Master, have invited
me to step out in faith. Eagerly, I take the leap. My feet
wet, I walk out to You standing there, waiting for me. But
then my focus veers away. My eyes see the waves roiling
beneath me. I feel the wind spraying salt water on my
face. My vision starts to blur, and the next thing I know,
I'm sinking in fear. I cry out for You to save me. And that's
what I'm doing right now in this moment, Lord—asking You
to give me the strength to turn from my fears and walk
forward in faith. Give me the power and peace I need to
stay focused on You and You alone. Amen.

VOICES RAISED IN PRAISE

Raise the voice of joy to God. . . . Come and see what God has done. . . . He changed the sea into dry land. They passed through the river on foot. There we were full of joy in Him. . . . We went through fire and through water. But You brought us out into a place where we have much more than we need. . . . Honor and thanks be to God!

PSALM 66:1, 5–6, 12, 20 NLV

. . . .

I may sometimes go through some rough patches, Lord, but somehow You always get me out. You make a way where there seems to be no way. You do the impossible when I'm between a rock and a hard place. You rescue me in a way that is so far beyond what I could have ever dreamed or imagined. And somehow, in the process, I end up better off than I was before! So I'm raising my voice of joy to You, Lord. Thank You for all You have done and continue to do in my life. All my love, honor, and thanks go to You. In Jesus' name I praise, amen.

Day 225

SIDELINES

*God's amazing grace be with you! God's robust
peace! . . . Stay calm; mind your own business;
do your own job. You've heard all this from us before,
but a reminder never hurts. We want you living in
a way that will command the respect of outsiders,
not lying around sponging off your friends.*

1 THESSALONIANS 1:1; 4:11–12 MSG

I don't know where I'd be, Lord, if it weren't for You and the grace and peace You so willingly pour down on me. For that peace is just what I need to follow Your lead, to be an example to others who are walking Your way. Help me, Lord, to stay calm, to remember that You love me, will always be here for me, and will forever care for me. Give me the strength to mind my own business, to do my own work, to live in such a way that You and Your Son will be glorified, that people will see His light instead of me, that He will "move into the center, while I slip off to the sidelines" (John 3:30 MSG). In Jesus' name, amen.

Day 226

HAPPY IN HOPE

Hold on to whatever is good. Love each other. . . .
Show respect for each other. . . . Work for the Lord
with a heart full of love for Him. Be happy in your
hope. Do not give up when trouble comes. Do not
let anything stop you from praying. Share what you
have with Christian brothers who are in need. Give
meals and a place to stay to those who need it.
ROMANS 12:9–13 NLV

Lord, I want to become the woman You designed me to be.
One of the spirit and not the flesh. So I'm going to focus on
all things good. I'm going to love and respect whomever I
meet. I'm going to work for You with all my heart. And I'll
be ecstatically happy because I have hope—in You, Your
kingdom, Your promises, Your precepts, and Your Word.
Such hope will keep me joyful and spiritually alive—even
in the midst of trouble. For I'll know You are with me
now and forever. And as I walk Your way, I'll find myself
just where You want me: happily serving those in need,
knowing that as I do so, I'm really serving You. In Jesus'
name, amen.

Day 227

THE BIG HELP

*I will lift up my eyes to the mountains. Where
will my help come from? My help comes from the
Lord, Who made heaven and earth. He will not let
your feet go out from under you. He Who watches
over you will not sleep. Listen, He Who watches
over Israel will not close his eyes or sleep.*
PSALM 121:1–4 NLV

Walking along the road of life, Lord, I often discover that
my focus is more on where I'll land than on where I actually am. But You have advised me, Lord, to live in the
present, not the future. So today I lift my eyes up to You,
Your mountains, Your heights. For You, the Creator and
caretaker of all, are all the help I need. You will not let
me trip up. You're the one who watches over me when I
sleep. In fact, You, my defender, never close Your eyes.
Be my lookout, my ever-vigilant protector. Keep me from
losing my way, from losing my courage, from losing my
peace. Lord, You are the one who holds me and mine in
Your hands forevermore. Amen.

Day 228

OPEN WIDE

Sing aloud to God our Strength! Shout for joy. . . .
You called in distress and I delivered you; I answered
you in the secret place of thunder; I tested you at
the waters of Meribah. . . . I am the Lord your God,
Who brought you up out of the land of Egypt. Open
your mouth wide and I will fill it. . . . Oh, that My people
would listen to Me, that Israel would walk in My ways!
PSALM 81:1, 7, 10, 13 AMPC

From You, Lord, I get the strength to overcome. To You, I shout for joy. Because whenever I call, Lord, You answer. When I am in need, You provide an answer. You are the one who continually rescues me. You part the sea so I can flee my foes. You subdue rulers so I can find my way to freedom in You. When I am hungry, You fill my mouth with food. When I am thirsty, You provide water from a rock. My joy lies in following You, obeying You, listening to You. For only when I walk in Your way am I on the right road to joy and Your kingdom. Amen.

Day 229

CLEAR AND OPEN

I have taught you in the way of skillful and godly Wisdom [which is comprehensive insight into the ways and purposes of God]; I have led you in paths of uprightness. When you walk, your steps shall not be hampered [your path will be clear and open]; and when you run, you shall not stumble. Take firm hold of instruction, do not let go; guard her, for she is your life.
PROVERBS 4:11–13 AMPC

. . . .

The more I get to know You, Lord, the more I learn in Your Word, the more the peace within me grows. For Your wisdom, instruction, guidance, and direction are what help me find boundaries, borders, blockages, and breakthroughs. Just learning Your many names gives me insight into who You are and who You are growing me to be—a gentle, patient, strong, and peaceful woman of God in Christ. So, Lord, as I continue walking along the way, with You by my side, I know my pathway will be clear and open. Give me the map You would have me follow. In Jesus' name, amen.

Day 230

A SPECIAL PLACE

Do not let your hearts be troubled (distressed, agitated).
You believe in and adhere to and trust in and rely on
God; believe in and adhere to and trust in and rely
also on Me. In My Father's house there are many
dwelling places (homes). If it were not so, I would
have told you; for I am going away to prepare a place
for you. . . . Where I am going, you know the way.
JOHN 14:1–2, 4 AMPC

Some days the woes, worries, and what-ifs come tumbling upon me, Lord. I get weighted down by this world so easily. And then I remember Your words. You've told me not to let my heart and mind be troubled but to trust in You, to lean on and rely on God. You've made it clear that You have a place for me in Father God's house. A room that You have prepared—just for me! I know the way there, so I'm running to You, Lord. Lift me up to that room, the one where I'll find You. That secret place of joy, where all my troubles melt away as I melt into You. Amen.

FAN THE FLAMES OF LOVE

*Get along among yourselves, each of you doing your
part. . . . Gently encourage the stragglers, and reach
out for the exhausted. . . . Be patient with each person,
attentive to individual needs. . . . Don't snap at each other.
Look for the best in each other, and always do your best
to bring it out. Be cheerful no matter what; pray all the
time; thank God no matter what happens. This is the
way God wants you who belong to Christ Jesus to live.*

1 THESSALONIANS 5:13–18 MSG

One way to maintain my peace, within and without, God,
is to be like Jesus. But for that, I'll definitely need Your
unerring wisdom and supernatural assistance. Help me to
do that work You've put in my hands to do. Give me words
of encouragement to share with people who are exhausted
as well as the patience to persevere, allowing people to
find their way at their own pace. Most of all, Lord, help
me to look for the best in others, not the worst. Help me
to find Your light within each human being. Then give
me the words that will fan their flames of love. In Jesus'
name I serve and pray. Amen.

FROM SORROW TO SOLUTION

The king said to me, Why do you look sad. . . ?
This is nothing but sorrow of heart. Then I was
very much afraid. . . . The king said to me, For
what do you ask? So I prayed to the God of heaven.
And I said to [him]. . .I ask that you will send me
to Judah. . . . And the king granted what I asked,
for the good hand of my God was upon me.
NEHEMIAH 2:2, 4–5, 8 AMPC

. . . .

When I am sad, Lord, when my heart is filled with sorrow, give me courage and allay my fears. Give me the words to speak to You so that I can get out from under my cloud of emotions and into the light of Your truth. Prompt me to pray, to lay out my concerns and worries before You. Help me seek Your will. Whether my prayer is long or short, spoken or silent, hear my words. Tell me what You would have me say or do. Show me which direction to go. For in You alone do I find the path to take, the courage and joy to go forward, walking with Your good hand upon me. Amen.

Day 233

HEART SET

*"If you set your heart on God and reach out to him,
if you scrub your hands of sin and refuse to entertain
evil in your home. . . you'll forget your troubles. . . .
Your world will be washed in sunshine, every
shadow dispersed by dawn. Full of hope, you'll relax,
confident again; you'll look around, sit back, and
take it easy. Expansive, without a care in the world,
you'll be hunted out by many for your blessing."*

JOB 11:13–14, 16–19 MSG

. . . .

My troubles have been weighing me down, Lord, keeping
me anxious, afraid, distracted. I'm so full of worry that
I'm neither walking forward or backward. I'm stuck in
this one spot. I need hope, Lord—hope that things will get
better. That someday all my confusion, woes, and fears will
drop away. That peace will then follow. For now, Lord, I'm
going to do what I can from my end. I'm setting my heart
on and reaching out to You, embracing good and rejecting
evil. For when I do, Your Word tells me my troubles will
soon be forgotten, as if they never existed. As hope will
once more reign, I'll be able to relax in You. Amen.

Day 234

NEVER ALONE

"The Father. . .will give you another Helper, to be with you forever. . . . I will not leave you as orphans; I will come to you. . . . If anyone loves me, he will keep my word, and my Father will love him, and we will come to him and make our home with him. . . . Peace I leave with you. . . . Let not your hearts be troubled."
JOHN 14:16, 18, 23, 27 ESV

There are times, Jesus, when I feel all alone. When it seems as if everyone has deserted me. I reach out, but no one is there—except for You. Thank You for promising to never leave me. For coming when I call You. For providing me with Your Spirit, the helper who takes my moans and groans and translates them into a prayer for God's ear. Because I love You and keep Your Word, You and the Spirit have made a home within me. What peace I find in You. What joy it gives my heart to know You will always be here with me. In Your name I pray and praise, amen.

ANSWERS ALREADY
ON THEIR WAY

This is the confidence (the assurance, the privilege of boldness) which we have in Him: [we are sure] that if we ask anything (make any request) according to His will (in agreement with His own plan), He listens to and hears us. And if (since) we [positively] know that He listens to us in whatever we ask, we also know [with settled and absolute knowledge] that we have. . .the requests made of Him.

1 JOHN 5:14–15 AMPC

It's amazing, Lord, how You walk with me through every situation in my life. How I am never alone but have You, the Creator of the universe, helping me every step of the way. For You have made it clear that if I ask for anything that agrees with Your Word, will, and way, You will not only hear my request but grant it! The certainty of that promise gives me great confidence and peace of mind. So here I am today, Lord, coming to You in prayer. Help me make sure that my requests are aligned with Your desire for me. Then help me rest in assurance, confident that You have heard my requests and that Your answers are already on their way. In Jesus' name I pray, amen.

Day 236

HOW BEAUTIFUL

How beautiful are the places where You live, O Lord of all! My soul wants and even becomes weak from wanting to be in the house of the Lord. My heart and my flesh sing for joy to the living God. Even the bird has found a home. The swallow has found a nest for herself where she may lay her young at Your altars, O Lord of all, my King and my God.
PSALM 84:1–3 NLV

. . . .

Where You live, Lord, must be amazing. I cannot even wrap my mind around what it might look like. Greater than the Taj Mahal. More amazing than the Grand Canyon. More beautiful than a Caribbean island. Wherever You are, in heaven or on earth, my soul longs to meet You, to be with You. There's no place I desire to be more than where You are. For You accept the humblest and simplest of creatures. When I, Your daughter, come to You, I feel like a princess in a palace. For in You, my Father and King, is where I find my real home. Where love, warmth, joy, and wonder rise up to greet me. As I follow Your light, I enter in, oh Lord, and bow at Your throne. Amen.

Day 237

NEVERTHELESS

They anointed David king over Israel, according to the word of the LORD by Samuel. And David and all Israel went to Jerusalem, that is, Jebus, where the Jebusites were. . . . The inhabitants of Jebus said to David, "You will not come in here." Nevertheless, David took the stronghold of Zion, that is, the city of David. . . . And David lived in the stronghold; therefore it was called the city of David.
1 CHRONICLES 11:3–5, 7 ESV

. . . .

Lord, I refuse to lose my peace. No matter how bad a situation looks, I know how well and quickly You can turn things around. No matter how many people try to dissuade me, force me out, talk over me, or criticize me, I'm hanging on to You, taking my cues and confidence from You. Because no matter how bad or hopeless things may seem or look, I know that for each one of Your children, You have a "nevertheless" up Your sleeve. And it's that "nevertheless" I look for with great anticipation and excitement. In Jesus' name, amen.

Day 238

JOY RUNNING OVER

I am the Vine and you are the branches. Get your life from Me. Then I will live in you and you will give much fruit. You can do nothing without Me. . . . If you get your life from Me and My Words live in you, ask whatever you want. It will be done for you. . . . I have told you these things so My joy may be in you and your joy may be full.
JOHN 15:5, 7, 11 NLV

. . . .

You, Jesus, are so precious. It's in You that I find my source of love, light, and life. For I can do nothing—and *am* nothing—without You. You feed me, nourish me, and give me the power to follow Your commandments. To love the Father with all my heart, mind, soul, and strength. And to love others as I love myself. Help me, Lord, to live my life *in* You, to obey Your teachings. For when I do, You will not only live in *me* but will grant me whatever I ask. Thank You for the joy this brings—Yours in me, and mine running over! In Your name I pray, amen.

Day 239

AN ENORMOUS ASK

"Do not worry about your life. Do not worry about what you are going to eat and drink. Do not worry about what you are going to wear. Is not life more important than food? Is not the body more important than clothes? Look at the birds in the sky. They do not plant seeds. They do not gather grain. . . . Yet your Father in heaven feeds them! Are you not more important than the birds?"
MATTHEW 6:25–26 NLV

. . . .

Lord, Your Word tells me not to worry about food and clothing or anything else that's going on (or not going on) in my life. On some days that feels like an enormous task. Yet still Your Word stands. And still I must follow it. So, Lord, every morning, greet me with a kiss and a good word, one I can carry in my heart and mind through my day. By midafternoon, Lord, show me what You would have me do to help another. And in the evening, Lord, as I lie on my bed, remind me of my blessings as I fall asleep in Your arms. Amen.

Day 240

PEACE-FILLED LIVING

*Pray and give thanks for those who make trouble for
you. Yes, pray for them instead of talking against them.
Be happy with those who are happy. Be sad with those
who are sad. Live in peace with each other. Do not act
or think with pride. Be happy to be with poor people.
Keep yourself from thinking you are so wise. . . .
As much as you can, live in peace with all men.*
ROMANS 12:14–16, 18 NLV

. . . .

The people of this world have become so contentious, Lord.
It seems to be a continuous battleground of disagreements.
And I know this is not Your way, for spiteful comebacks
suck the joy and peace right out of life. Lord, I want to take
the higher road. So give me the words to pray for those
who make trouble for me. Help me not to say anything
bad against them but to thank You for bringing them into
my life. Help me to treat others with compassion and to
be the peacemaker in all situations. In other words, Lord
Jesus, give me the strength, courage, and fortitude to be
more like You—acquainted with sorrow yet, in praying
and serving others, transformed by joy. In Your name I
pray, amen.

Day 241

WOES IN TOW

Keep your foot [give your mind to what you are doing] when you go. . .to the house of God. For to draw near to hear and obey is better than to give the sacrifice of fools. . . . Be not rash with your mouth, and let not your heart be hasty to utter a word before God. For God is in heaven, and you are on earth; therefore let your words be few.
ECCLESIASTES 5:1–2 AMPC

I have so many things on my mind, Lord, that any peace I may have had at some point has flown right out the window. As a result, my focus and concentration are way off. So I'm making my way back to You, Lord, with all my woes in tow. I'm going to draw so near to You that I can hear You breathing and Your heart beating. Then I'm going to snuggle up and take in the beauty and wonder of Your presence, the warmth of Your light, the peace of Your mind. Here, this close with You, my words will be few but my love abundant. In Jesus' name, amen.

Day 242

GENTLE STRENGTH

How happy are those who live in Your house! They are always giving thanks to You. How happy is the man whose strength is in You and in whose heart are the roads to Zion! As they pass through the dry valley of Baca, they make it a place of good water. The early rain fills the pools with good also. They go from strength to strength. Every one of them stands before God.

PSALM 84:4–7 NLV

. . . .

The more time I spend with You, Jesus—studying Your Word, praying Your way, absorbing Your truths, following Your will—the stronger I seem to become. At each point, with each trial, I learn more, grow more, and find myself closer and closer to You. Yet at the same time my strength is increasing, the gentler I have become and the more I find peace, even in the midst of trial. All this gives me such joy. The unshakable kind. The joy that makes my foundation in You so firm. Thank You, Lord, for being there—everywhere I look. Everywhere I love. Everywhere I roam, from strength to strength, I'm home in You. Amen.

Day 243

BEGINNING NOW

*With God rests my salvation and my glory; He is my Rock
of unyielding strength and impenetrable hardness,
and my refuge is in God! Trust in, lean on, rely on, and
have confidence in Him at all times, you people; pour out
your hearts before Him. God is a refuge for us (a fortress
and a high tower). Selah [pause, and calmly think of that]!*
PSALM 62:7–8 AMPC

I have so many things on my mind, Lord, and they're sapping me of my strength. For each one carries with it a potential concern. Yet since concerns are what I'm *not* to be focused on, I've been trying to tamp down all my worries. Unfortunately, today I feel like all my frets have imploded within me, knocking me off balance. So I'm running to You, Lord, my high tower. I'm pouring out to You all the worries that have been building up inside me, stealing my peace, darkening my heart. One by one, I leave my woes at Your feet, beginning right now, in this moment. Amen.

Day 244

BIRTHING JOY

"When a woman gives birth, she has a hard time, there's no getting around it. But when the baby is born, there is joy in the birth. This new life in the world wipes out memory of the pain. The sadness you have right now is similar to that pain, but the coming joy is also similar. When I see you again, you'll be full of joy, and it will be a joy no one can rob from you."
JOHN 16:22–23 MSG

. . . .

It's so true, Lord! When a woman is pregnant, she and her body go through a lot. First she's happy she's going to have a baby. Then she may have morning sickness, become physically awkward, and have to get up at night to relieve herself. And that's just the prelude to the overture of pain that comes with giving birth. Yet when she holds that baby, that gift of life in her arms, the love she has for that child eventually erases all the prior pain. And it's the same with lots of other things in life, Lord. I may have hard times, but because You're with me through the trials, I know I'll find the joy I desire in You—from pain to pleasure, from beginning to end. Amen.

Day 245

PEACE RESTORED

May the Lord direct your hearts into [realizing and showing] the love of God. . . . And as for you, brethren, do not become weary or lose heart in doing right [but continue in well-doing without weakening]. . . . Now may the Lord of peace Himself grant you His peace (the peace of His kingdom) at all times and in all ways [under all circumstances and conditions, whatever comes].

2 THESSALONIANS 3:5, 13, 16 AMPC

. . . .

Some days, Lord, I feel so frustrated. I keep putting love and compassion out there in the world, whenever and wherever I can, and I often get back nothing but silence, suspicion, or disdain. I try to live my life as You would have me live it, doing the right thing, helping others, but it's hard to stay up and in the light when so many people are so down and in the dark. That's why I'm coming to You, Lord, to restore my peace by asking You to direct my heart toward whom You would have me help and to leave the results of my efforts to You. Help me, no matter what my circumstances, to keep Your peace in me. Amen.

Day 246

HAPPY IN JESUS

O Lord God of all, hear my prayer. . . . Look upon our safe-covering, O God. And look upon the face of Your chosen one. For a day in Your house is better than a thousand outside. . . . For the Lord God is a sun and a safe-covering. . . . He holds back nothing good from those who walk in the way that is right. O Lord of all, how happy is the man who trusts in You!

PSALM 84:8–12 NLV

. . . .

After a week in the world, Lord, I run to Your house of worship. I run to join Your other children in prayer and praise as we lift our eyes and hearts to You. Thank You, Lord, for keeping me safe, looking out for me from Monday to Saturday. Thank You for coming into our presence when we come to Your house. Every minute spent there is so precious. For I see Your love and light in those who worship with me, Lord. We happily trust You to help us, to meet with us, to keep us strong as we endeavor to serve You. Amen.

Day 247

COMING AND GOING

The Lord watches over you. The Lord is your safe cover at your right hand. The sun will not hurt you during the day and the moon will not hurt you during the night. The Lord will keep you from all that is sinful. He will watch over your soul. The Lord will watch over your coming and going, now and forever.
PSALM 121:5–8 NLV

. . . .

I love the idea of You watching over me, Lord, covering me from all dangers within and without. Because of You and Your 24-7 vigilance, I need not worry about being harmed during the day or when I sleep at night. You are a massive shield of protection that surrounds me—no matter where I am or who I am with or what I am doing. I need no special tool, phone, book, computer, or electronic device to call You or reach You. No, I have a direct line to You through prayer. So help me keep that in mind, Lord, as I go through my day. May the idea that You are watching me now and will do so forever help me not only keep my peace but revel in it, for You are the source of calm I yearn for. In Jesus' name, amen.

Day 248

COMPLETED WITH JOY

Forget about deciding what's right for each other. . . .
God's kingdom isn't a matter of what you put in
your stomach, for goodness' sake. It's what God does
with your life as he sets it right, puts it together,
and completes it with joy. Your task is to single-
mindedly serve Christ. Do that and you'll kill two
birds with one stone: pleasing the God above you
and proving your worth to the people around you.
ROMANS 14:13, 17–18 MSG

Jesus, there are so many traditions, rules, and methods people say should be used to serve You, love You, pray to You, worship You, and more. It's mind-boggling. All I want is to follow what You would have me do. So help me to focus on You more than any other thing. Help me to dive deeply into Your Word for direction. To concentrate on serving You and You alone. For I know when I do, the Father will use me as He desires and fill my life with joy. What more can a woman ask but to please Father God and be of worth to those around her? In Jesus' name, amen.

A SOLUTION UNIMAGINABLE

*The Philistines came up again. . . . David asked the Lord
what he should do. And the Lord said, "Do not go up,
but go around behind them and come at them in front of the
balsam trees. When you hear the sound of their steps in
the tops of the balsam trees, then hurry to fight, for then
the Lord will have gone out before you to destroy the
Philistine army." David did just as the Lord told him.*

2 Samuel 5:22–25 NLV

. . . .

Nothing like being challenged once more by the same old
enemy, Lord. And this time, in my uncertainty, I feel as if
I have no firm footing. How many times will I have to fight
the same foe, Lord? When will I ever regain my peace?
And that's when I realize You will most likely come up with
a battle plan or solution I'd never dreamed or imagined.
For Your thoughts and plans, Lord, are not the same as the
thoughts and plans I entertain. But it *is* in You that I do
trust. So here I come, Lord, asking Your help once more.
Tell me what to do against this latest challenge, and I'll do
just as You say. In Jesus' name, amen.

LORD KNOWS

The heart knows its own bitterness, and no stranger shares its joy. . . . In the reverent and worshipful fear of the Lord there is strong confidence, and His children shall always have a place of refuge. . . . A calm and undisturbed mind and heart are the life and health of the body. . . . Wisdom rests [silently] in the mind and heart of him who has understanding.
PROVERBS 14:10, 26, 30, 33 AMPC

Only You can fully understand and empathize with the sorrow I bear in my heart, Lord. And yet at the same time, only You can fully understand, know, and take part in the joy I experience as well. Whether joyful or sad, I know You are with me, tending to me, caring for me, crying or laughing with me. In You I find shelter from the storms of life. You give me the peace I crave. You calm my heart and quiet my spirit. Give me the wisdom, Lord, to run to You whether I am in tears or rolling with laughter. Share my life, sorrows, and joys, Lord, as I live and move in You. Amen.

Day 251

THE FIRST THING

*The first thing I want you to do is pray. Pray every
way you know how, for everyone you know.
Pray especially for rulers and their governments to rule
well so we can be quietly about our business of living
simply, in humble contemplation. This is the way our
Savior God wants us to live. . . . What I want mostly is
for men to pray—not shaking angry fists at enemies
but raising holy hands to God. And I want women to
get in there with the men in humility before God.*

1 TIMOTHY 2:1–3, 8–9 MSG

Prayer is such a powerful tool and an essential component of my relationship with You, Lord. For all endeavors, all plans and challenges, seem to begin with words. Good words. Yet I know at times that I'm lax in my duty to pray. Help me change that now, Lord. To really get back into prayer, conversation with You, and go deep. Help me also, Lord, to pray for *all* people, including politicians, even if I neither respect nor agree with them. For then we believers can live in peace and quiet, going about our day to live and serve You. In Jesus' name, amen.

Day 252

FROM SADNESS TO GLADNESS

"You're going to be in deep mourning while the godless world throws a party. You'll be sad, very sad, but your sadness will develop into gladness. . . . This is what I want you to do: Ask the Father for whatever is in keeping with the things I've revealed to you. Ask in my name, according to my will, and he'll most certainly give it to you. Your joy will be a river overflowing its banks!"
JOHN 16:20, 23–24 MSG

. . . .

I'm looking to You for direction, Jesus. I want to walk in Your way, according to Your will. You are the way and truth and life. When You were here on earth and now while You're in heaven, You know exactly what's going to happen in my life and why. You have said my path lies in You. Show me, Jesus, what You would have me pray for, what You would have me ask for. Align my heart, mind, and desires so they are in line with Yours. For I know that as You do so, my "sadness will develop into gladness." My joy will overflow its banks. In Your precious name I pray, amen.

Day 253

ALL MY TOMORROWS

Deceit is in the heart of those who devise evil, but those who plan peace have joy. . . . Anxiety in a man's heart weighs him down, but a good word makes him glad.
PROVERBS 12:20, 25 ESV

You, Lord, are a planner. You know exactly how everything is going to work out for me. Many times I've wished I knew what was going to happen. Yet at other times, I'm glad I cannot see into my future. Regardless of how I feel about knowing or not knowing, You've hidden my tomorrows from me. And as I walk this earth, I'm trusting that You will continue to be with me, for me, and in me. That You will forever be with me, loving and protecting me till the end of time. Because I trust You, I can rest in You. I can put all my tomorrows in Your hands. That leaves me free to plan peace. To find ways that I can soothe others. So plant some good words in my head, Lord. Then tell me who needs to hear them to so I can plant the peace and spread the joy I find in You. Amen.

Day 254

JOY-GIVER

Lord God of all, powerful Lord, who is like You?
All around You we see how faithful You are. You rule
over the rising sea. When its waves rise, You quiet
them. . . . You have a strong arm. Your hand is
powerful. . . . Your throne stands on what is right
and fair. Loving-kindness and truth go before You.
How happy are the people who know the sound of joy!
PSALM 89:8–9, 13–15 NLV

. . . .

I'm amazed, Lord, at how faithful You are to me. Especially
when I have erred, slipped up, or been unfaithful to You.
Thank You, God, that You are in control of not just *my* life
but of everyone's lives, as well as this world's ebb and
flow. That gives me hope, Lord. And hope opens the door
to joy—not just for me but for everyone, everything, all
that You have created. Nothing can overpower You, Lord.
So I'm clinging to You. I'm waiting for You, Your justice,
Your peace, Your favor, Your strength, Your saving grace.
And as I wait, I'm going to trust in You, my joy-giver. For
in You is goodness. In You is calm. In You, I'm sound and
saved. Amen.

Day 255

MIRRORING GOD'S TRANQUILITY

Every man to whom God has given riches and possessions, and the power to enjoy them and to accept his appointed lot and to rejoice in his toil—this is the gift of God [to him]. For he shall not much remember [seriously] the days of his life, because God [Himself] answers and corresponds to the joy of his heart [the tranquility of God is mirrored in him].

ECCLESIASTES 5:19–20 AMPC

. . . .

Too often, Lord, I find that the bad things that are happening in this world are overshadowing the blessings You have given me. That's put me in a very discontented state. That means I need to change my focus and attitude, Lord—and I need to do that right now. But I cannot do so without Your help. I want to do more than just focus on the blessings, all the riches and possessions You've given me, as well as the joys of working in and for You. For what I desire even more, Lord, is to mirror Jesus. To nourish the peace and joy I have in You all the days of my life. In Jesus' name, amen.

Day 256

THE MORNING STAR RISES

We have the prophetic word. . . . You will do well to pay close attention to it as to a lamp shining in a dismal (squalid and dark) place, until the day breaks through [the gloom] and the Morning Star rises (comes into being) in your hearts. . . . I waited patiently and expectantly for the Lord. . . . [She proudly said] I am my beloved's, and his desire is toward me! . . . Come, my beloved!
2 Peter 1:19; Psalm 40:1; Song of Solomon 7:10–11 AMPC

. . . .

Be with me, Lord Jesus, as I enter Your Word. Help me not just to read it but to take it in, absorb it, and allow it to work its way into my life. Let the light and power of Your Word break through the gloom within me until You rise up and come into being within my heart, changing whatever sorrows that linger into joy. You are my bright Morning Star, Jesus. For You I patiently wait. It is Your presence I expect to change me from the inside out, letter by letter, word by word. You are my beloved. Desire me as I desire You. Come, Jesus. Come now. Amen.

A HANDFUL OF QUIETNESS

I saw that all toil and all skill in work come from a man's envy of his neighbor. This also is vanity and a striving after wind. The fool folds his hands and eats his own flesh. Better is a handful of quietness than two hands full of toil and a striving after wind.
ECCLESIASTES 4:4–6 ESV

Trying to keep up with the Joneses is exhausting, Lord, and can go on forever. And that's not what I want to spend my life doing, for there's no peace to be found in such a competition. I'd much rather be working for You and striving for the things You want me to reach for— things such as peace, courage, patience, love, forgiveness, and compassion. So help me, Lord, to strike a balance between using my hands to meet the needs of the flesh and the needs of the spirit. And as I do so, Lord, help me to be more content with a handful of quietness in Your presence than clutching all the work I can handle with my only gain afterward being a fleeting pleasure soon blown away by the wind. Amen.

Day 258

WALKING ON AIR

*Blessed are the people who know the passwords of praise, who shout on parade in the bright presence of G*OD*. Delighted, they dance all day long; they know who you are, what you do—they can't keep it quiet! Your vibrant beauty has gotten inside us—you've been so good to us! We're walking on air! All we are and have we owe to G*OD*, Holy God of Israel, our King!*
PSALM 89:15–18 MSG

At times, Lord, I can't see the forest for the trees; I can't see the good within the bad. Although that seems the natural way of man (and woman), I know that's not how You want us to view the world. For when we see only the perils and darkness, we miss the safety and light. So help change me, Lord. Help me focus more on the showers with blessings, the good, the light. Prompt me to dance and shout in praise. Remind me of who You are, what You've done. Fill me with such joy and delight that I'm lifted way above the earth, praising You all the day. In Jesus' name I pray, amen.

Day 259

SLOW TO ANGER

*Then the Lord passed in front of him and proclaimed:
Yahweh—Yahweh is a compassionate and gracious God,
slow to anger and rich in faithful love and truth. . . . Tear
your hearts, not just your clothes, and return to the Lord
your God. For He is gracious and compassionate, slow
to anger, rich in faithful love. . . . A hot-tempered man
stirs up conflict, but a man slow to anger calms strife.*
Exodus 34:6; Joel 2:13; Proverbs 15:18 HCSB

. . . .

You, Lord, are a God of peace. That was seen in a big way
when You allowed Your Son to die so that I could live
with and love You forever. That's an *amazing* amount of
compassion and love You have shown for Your oftentimes
wayward children. Yet that's exactly the kind of peace,
love, and compassion I want in my own life. I want to be a
woman slow to anger, someone who doesn't create strife
but instead brings calm. Protect me, Lord, as I endeavor
to be like You. Amen.

Day 260

JOY-MAKERS

We who are strong [in our convictions and of robust faith] ought to bear with the failings and the frailties and the tender scruples of the weak; [we ought to help carry the doubts and qualms of others] and not to please ourselves. Let each one of us make it a practice to please (make happy) his neighbor for his good and for his true welfare, to edify him [to strengthen him and build him up spiritually].

ROMANS 15:1–2 AMPC

Lord, I feel so blessed to be aware of the role that joy plays in my life. But this joy is not just for me alone. This is something that I can use to help others. So each day, Lord, as I hope in You, count my blessings, and revel in the joy of You, remind me to help others—those who are not as strong in their faith. Help me to please You by helping to please them, to make them happy, to bring a smile to their faces, to encourage them, to build them up in their spirits. In other words, Lord, use me to spread Your joy from here to eternity! In Jesus' name I pray, amen.

GETTING ALONG

Work at getting along with each other and with God.
Otherwise you'll never get so much as a glimpse of God.
Make sure no one gets left out of God's generosity. Keep
a sharp eye out for weeds of bitter discontent. A thistle
or two gone to seed can ruin a whole garden in no time.
Watch out for the Esau syndrome: trading away God's
lifelong gift in order to satisfy a short-term appetite.
HEBREWS 12:14–16 MSG

. . . .

Lord, I want to live a life where I not only get along with people but go the extra mile to help them. You emphasize that I am to love You with all I am and love others as I love myself. You have created love to be Your children's pathway to peace. And that's the road I want to be on. But some people, Lord, are a bit hard to love. So please fill my heart with love, my soul with peace, and my lips with encouraging words as I reach out to all around me, in honor of Your Son, Jesus. Amen.

Day 262

TRUE HAPPINESS

Then Haman went out that day glad and with joy in
his heart. But when he saw Mordecai at the king's gate,
and when he did not stand up or show any fear in front
of him, Haman was filled with anger. . . . For the Jews
it was a time of joy and happiness and honor. In every
part of the nation and in every city where the king's law
had come, there was happiness and joy for the Jews.
ESTHER 5:9; 8:16–17 NLV

It's interesting, Lord, how I need to be sure of my source of joy. Does the joy I find in my life come from the deep well of knowing You, seeking You, and abiding in You? Or does my joy come from the shallow stream that eddies around my self-pride, honor, and worldly ambitions? The test seems to be that if my joy comes from the deep well of pleasing You instead of the shallow well of pleasing myself and the world, my happiness will not be fleeting but a deep, constant, and abiding joy. Help me seek my joy and happiness in You alone, Lord. For then I will find the everlasting gladness that comes only by living for and in You. Amen.

UNANXIOUS AND UNINTIMIDATED

What matters is not your outer appearance. . .but your inner disposition. Cultivate inner beauty, the gentle, gracious kind that God delights in. The holy women of old were beautiful before God that way, and were good, loyal wives to their husbands. Sarah, for instance, taking care of Abraham, would address him as "my dear husband." You'll be true daughters of Sarah if you do the same, unanxious and unintimidated.

1 PETER 3:3–6 MSG

How freeing it is, Lord, knowing that You aren't concerned with my outer appearance, that I don't have to dress up to impress or please You. For that's only surface beauty. But I do need Your guidance in how to be beautiful on the inside. So lead me, Lord, to the verses that will guide me to a place at rest in You. There I will sit at Your feet and take in Your wisdom. There, Lord, teach me how to be at ease, confident and unintimidated. Teach me how to be just like Jesus. In His name I pray, amen.

JOY IN THE JOURNEY

*Everything that was written in the Holy Writings
long ago was written to teach us. By not giving up,
God's Word gives us strength and hope. Now the God
Who helps you not to give up and gives you strength
will help you think so you can please each other as
Christ Jesus did. Then all of you together can thank
the God and Father of our Lord Jesus Christ.*
ROMANS 15:4–6 NLV

. . . .

Thank You, Lord, for the Old Testament writings that teach me about You, Your Son, Your Spirit—and myself. The stories that teach me so many valuable lessons, including the one about Joseph. So many things were against him, Lord. Yet even though he'd been sold into servitude, unjustly accused, and then jailed, Joseph continued to be positive, hopeful, and joyful—and so he prospered. For he knew You were with him *and* that although others had planned evil against him, You would use those same plans for his good (see Genesis 50:20)! Help me, Lord, to have that same trust that You're with me, that same assurance that all that happens—including the seemingly bad—will all work out for my good. For then I too will find joy and success in my journey with You. Amen.

THE GOD OF PEACE

*Now may the God of peace, who brought up from
the dead our Lord Jesus—the great Shepherd of the
sheep—with the blood of the everlasting covenant,
equip you with all that is good to do His will, working
in us what is pleasing in His sight, through Jesus Christ.
Glory belongs to Him forever and ever. Amen.*
HEBREWS 13:20–21 HCSB

Part of my peace, Lord, comes from knowing that whatever You call me to, You will also equip me for. And it's all because You are the God of peace, because You stop all the turmoil, assuage my fear, strengthen me against temptation, and fight for me against troublemakers. It is You, Lord—who had the supreme power to raise Jesus from the dead—who gives me the *real* rest, the true rest I need to take in You. It is while I rest in You and Your peace, in Your power and Your strength, that You do even more work within me. Thank You, Lord, for all the good You do for me. Amen.

SAFETY, SECURITY, AND GUIDANCE

*The Lord. . .heard my cry. He drew me up out of a
horrible pit [a pit of tumult and of destruction], out of
the miry clay (froth and slime), and set my feet upon a
rock, steadying my steps and establishing my goings.
And He has put a new song in my mouth, a song of praise
to our God. . . . Blessed (happy, fortunate, to be envied)
is the man who makes the Lord his refuge and trust.*
PSALM 40:1–4 AMPC

. . . .

Oh Lord, my God, You make my heart sing. For when I'm
in trouble and call out to You, You respond immediately.
You pull me out of peril, set my feet firmly on a rock, and
then steady my steps. You bless me with safety, security,
and guidance. And then, on top of all that, You put a new
song in my mouth so that I cannot help but praise You
from here to kingdom come! I truly am happy, overflowing
with joy, because I have You, Lord. Because I have made
You my shelter, my refuge from life's storms. In You, I put
all my trust. Thank You, Lord, for all these blessings and
more. Amen.

Day 267

WHAT "WORKS"

What good is it, my brothers, if someone says he has faith but does not have works? Can his faith save him? If a brother or sister is without clothes and lacks daily food and one of you says to them, "Go in peace, keep warm, and eat well," but you don't give them what the body needs, what good is it? In the same way faith, if it doesn't have works, is dead by itself.

JAMES 2:14–17 HCSB

. . . .

Lord, You have given me so much peace across the years that now I want to spread that peace, that calm, that assurance one can find only in You. I want to add works to my faith by helping others. But I'm not sure what those "works" might be. So I'm coming to You for help, for inspiration. Show me, Lord, what You would have me do, how You would have me serve You by coming alongside someone else. Show me where to begin. Give me the courage to reach out. In the meantime, I'll continue to pray and seek Your will, Your way, with my eyes wide open. In Jesus' name I pray, amen.

Day 268

JOIN IN THE CHALLENGE

*Peter answered Him, Lord, if it is You, command me to
come to You on the water. He said, Come! So Peter got
out of the boat and walked on the water, and he came
toward Jesus. But when he perceived and felt the strong
wind, he was frightened, and as he began to sink,
he cried out, Lord, save me [from death]! Instantly Jesus
reached out His hand and caught and held him.*
MATTHEW 14:28–31 AMPC

You, Jesus, have a way of taking Your followers out of their
comfort zones. First, You direct Your disciples to cross the
sea. The next thing they know, they're desperately trying
to ride out a storm. Yet before they even cry out for help,
You appear in a miraculous way, walking on the water. You
yell over their screams, telling them to be brave. Peter then
takes another challenge and begins to walk toward You.
But seeing the wind and waves, he cries out to You—and
immediately You grab hold of him. You, Lord, are the joy
I find in all my challenges. With my eyes on You, I can
do all things, knowing You'll be ready to catch me. Amen.

TAKING IT IN

"Job, are you listening? Have you noticed all this? Stop in your tracks! Take in God's miracle-wonders!" . . . I look up at your macro-skies, dark and enormous, your handmade sky-jewelry, moon and stars mounted in their settings.

JOB 37:14; PSALM 8:3 MSG

. . . .

Today, Lord, I have discord within and without, and I'm not sure why. There's really nothing I can put my finger on as the cause of this unease, but the feeling is there nevertheless. So I'm going to follow Your wisdom, Lord, which begins by opening up not just my mind but my ears. There's been so much chattering in my mind that it's no wonder I feel a bit disconnected at times. So I'm looking to open my eyes as well, within and without, to see what's around me. I'm going to stop all activity—working, playing, thinking, dreaming—and take in and appreciate all the beauty You have created, all the miracles You've wrought, all the universe You sustain, all the love and light You pour upon me. In Jesus' name, amen.

Day 270

FROM HOPE TO JOY AND PEACE

Isaiah says, "There will be One from the family of Jesse Who will be a leader over the people who are not Jews. Their hope will be in Him." Our hope comes from God. May He fill you with joy and peace because of your trust in Him. May your hope grow stronger by the power of the Holy Spirit. . . . May our God Who gives us peace, be with you all. Let it be so.
ROMANS 15:12–13, 33 NLV

My hope is bound up in You, Jesus. For You are the one I look to, the one I live for because You lead me through sun and shade. You build me up, strengthen me, encourage me, renew and refresh me. I trust You to get me through every wilderness wandering. And because of my hope and trust in You, God fills me with the joy and peace so lacking in this world. Help me, Lord, to lay myself open to You and Your way. To follow the leadings of the Spirit, to allow Him to have greater sway over my life, so that I will be stronger and better able to serve You with peace of mind and heart. Lord, let it be so. Amen.

BY FAITH

*Now faith is the assurance (the confirmation, the title
deed) of the things [we] hope for, being the proof of
things [we] do not see and the conviction of their reality
[faith perceiving as real fact what is not revealed to the
senses]. . . . By faith we understand that the worlds. . .
were framed. . .by the word of God, so that what we
see was not made out of things which are visible.*
HEBREWS 11:1, 3 AMPC

When stress knocks on my door, I soon find my faith taking
a walkabout. An instant later, my peace is running after it.
Then I'm left feeling like a quivering bowl of lime Jell-O,
shaking with doubts and anxieties. Lord, this is not at all
how You want me to live. So, Lord, fill me with Your presence as I slowly take this next breath and another and
another. As I seek You within, reveal Yourself, Your light,
Your warmth, Your love. Remind me that all is well. That
You will never leave or forsake me. That all I hope for is
already on its way to me through You, my Lord and Savior,
my hope and stay. Amen.

Day 272

CONSTANT CONVERSATION

*Many, O Lord my God, are the wonderful works which
You have done, and Your thoughts toward us; no one
can compare with You! If I should declare and speak of
them, they are too many to be numbered. . . . I delight
to do Your will, O my God; yes, Your law is within my
heart. . . . Let all those that seek and require You rejoice
and be glad in You. . .my Help and my Deliverer.*
PSALM 40:5, 8, 16–17 AMPC

. . . .

I don't just want You, Lord, but I seek You out, wherever I
am, whatever I'm doing. I'm in constant conversation with
You because I need You more than anything else in this
world and the next. There is no greater guide than You.
No greater power, force, refuge, strengthener. You don't
just help me, Lord; You deliver me. You get me out of so
many sticky situations, often ones that I myself have made.
Make me ever more aware of Your presence and my need
for You, Lord. In You I find all the joy I could ever hope
for or imagine. In Jesus' name, amen.

Day 273

SWEET PEACE

Wherever you find jealousy and fighting, there will be trouble and every other kind of wrong-doing. But the wisdom that comes from heaven is first of all pure. Then it gives peace. It is gentle and willing to obey. It is full of loving-kindness and of doing good. It has no doubts and does not pretend to be something it is not. Those who plant seeds of peace will gather what is right and good.

JAMES 3:16–18 NLV

. . . .

I need some pointers, Lord, on how to make good decisions. In the past, I have talked to family members, partners, coworkers, and friends about what I should do, where I should go, how I should serve. But I still feel so very lost, not quite sure where my true path is. Perhaps, Lord, I've been looking for advice in all the wrong places. Instead of asking my fellow humans, I should be asking You for advice. So here I am, Lord, looking for Your knowledge, for that perfect heavenly wisdom that not only gives me peace but prompts me to plant seeds of peace. Ah, sweet peace, free of fears and worries, is Your wisdom and way. Amen.

Day 274

FOREVER PRAYER

*"While I have been with [My followers] in the world,
I have kept them in the power of Your name. I have
kept watch over those You gave Me. . . . But now I
come to You, Father. I say these things while I am in
the world. In this way, My followers may have My joy
in their hearts. . . . I do not pray for these followers
only. I pray for those who will put their trust in Me."*
JOHN 17:12–13, 20 NLV

. . . .

At times, Jesus, I don't feel very loved or even lovable. I feel
unprotected, alone. And then, with all the strength I can
muster, I turn to You. I open Your Word. And there I find
the comfort, love, safety, and joy I long for. For You, Lord,
are watching over me. You keep me safe in the power of
God's name. And before You gave up Your life for mine, You
even prayed to God *for me!* I am one who lives with her trust
in You. And this prayer You prayed for me is still rising up
with the smoke of incense in the presence of God from the
hand of the angel (see Revelation 8:4). I'm overwhelmed,
Lord, with joy from and in You, my forever prayer. Amen.

NAME CALLING

"Woman," Jesus said to her, "why are you crying?
Who is it you are looking for?" Supposing He was
the gardener, she replied, "Sir, if you've removed Him,
tell me where you've put Him, and I will take Him away."
Jesus said, "Mary." Turning around, she said to Him
in Hebrew, "Rabbouni!"—which means "Teacher."
JOHN 20:15–16 HCSB

. . . .

Lord, I have had days when I couldn't find You. When wherever I looked, all our old familiar places seemed empty, bereft of Your presence, light, grace, love, kindness, and direction. I didn't know where to turn, how to reach You. I thought perhaps You were wearing a disguise. Or, much more likely, there was something wrong with my vision. My perception was off. Regardless of the reason, my peace was disturbed and my tears were about to flow. That's when I heard a voice ask, "Why is it you're crying? Who are you looking for?" And my answer was "Tell me where Jesus is. And I'll take Him away with me." Next thing I knew, You were calling my name. I heard and felt the love in Your voice. The scales fell away, and it was You I saw before me. Peace and joy once more were mine. Amen.

Day 276

PROTECTING ANGELS

He who dwells in the secret place of the Most High shall remain stable and fixed under the shadow of the Almighty [Whose power no foe can withstand]. I will say of the Lord, He is my Refuge and my Fortress, my God; on Him I lean and rely, and in Him I [confidently] trust! . . . He will cover you. . . . You shall not be afraid. . . .He will give His angels [especial] charge over you.
PSALM 91:1–2, 4, 5, 11 AMPC

When I'm not trusting You, Lord, worry and dread take all the joy out of my life. So when I'm in that dark place of fretting and fearing, lift me up to that secret place—Your presence. Only there will I find the safety and courage I need! For when I'm in that place, no one—within or without—can withstand Your power. Lord, my refuge and fortress, on You alone I'm leaning and relying. In You I'm putting all my trust. In You alone do I gain the strength and courage I need to face the day and find the joy that comes from knowing Your angels are watching over me. So be it! Amen!

Day 277

STANDING ON THE SHORE

Simon Peter announced, "I'm going fishing." The rest of them replied, "We're going with you." They went out and got in the boat. They caught nothing that night. When the sun came up, Jesus was standing on the beach, but they didn't recognize him. . . . He said, "Throw the net off the right side of the boat and see what happens." They did what he said. All of a sudden there were so many fish in it, they weren't strong enough to pull it in.
JOHN 21:3–4, 6 MSG

When I'm restless, anxious, afraid, impatient, confused, or frustrated, Lord, I find myself automatically going back to something familiar, something from my old life that once brought me comfort, hoping to regain my peace. Yet I soon discover that whenever I attempt anything without You, I come up empty. No matter how hard or how long I try or how much help I have, my endeavor without You bears no fruit. But then You appear on the scene, standing on the shore. You see me floundering in the sea. You, who appear to me a stranger, yell instructions. I obey. And my efforts pay off big-time! That's when I realize it's *You* standing on the shore. *You* are my blessing. *You* are my peace. *You* are my bounty. Amen.

Day 278

ENCAMPED IN HOPE

I saw the Lord constantly before me, for He is at my right hand that I may not be shaken or overthrown or cast down [from my secure and happy state]. Therefore my heart rejoiced and my tongue exulted exceedingly; moreover, my flesh also will dwell in hope [will encamp, pitch its tent, and dwell in hope]. . . . You have made known to me the ways of life; You will enrapture me [diffusing my soul with joy] with and in Your presence.
ACTS 2:25–26, 28 AMPC

. . . .

Lord Jesus, I want You constantly before me, beside me, within me. I want to see this world though Your eyes. In that way, I will never be shaken, be brought low, or struck with a worldly mindset. With You, I will stay safe and secure. I will find all the joy I can handle. I'm driving stakes into the ground of hope. There my tent will be pitched, stable, unmovable. There is where I will live this life—happy in Your home, in Your presence, where You'll fill my spirit and drip Your joy upon my soul. In Your love, Your strength, Your presence, and Your name I pray, amen.

BEING A BLESSING

Now finally, all of you should be like-minded and sympathetic, should love believers, and be compassionate and humble, not paying back evil for evil or insult for insult but, on the contrary, giving a blessing, since you were called for this, so that you can inherit a blessing.

1 PETER 3:8–9 HCSB

. . . .

On the whole, Lord, I'm not a very vengeful person, looking to hurt others, to pay them back for any wrong they did me. But I definitely need Your help in forgiving them. Lord, give me the courage to turn the other cheek, go the extra mile, give in addition to what has been taken. Some people may say that makes me a light touch, a patsy. I say it makes me more like You, Jesus—and a true person of peace. A person who sees others with compassion and love, who wants to help make the lives of others better. Lord, I want to be a blessing to all I meet. That sounds like a very tall order, but You have said that with You, I can do anything. So let's begin today, Lord. Who can I bless in Jesus' name? Amen.

Day 280

A STORY TO GLORY

What a beautiful thing, God, to give thanks, to sing an anthem to you, the High God! To announce your love each daybreak, sing your faithful presence all through the night. . . . You made me so happy, God. I saw your work and I shouted for joy. . . . My ears are filled with the sounds of promise: "Good people will prosper. . . . They'll grow tall in the presence of God, lithe and green, virile still in old age."

PSALM 92:1–2, 4, 11–14 MSG

When the world tries to drag me down into hopelessness, I'm going to fight back. I'm going to give thanks to You, Lord. I'm going to sing Your praises, proclaim how much You love me. I'm going to keep You with me throughout the day and then sing about how faithful You are to me at night. All my joy and happiness are bound up in Your promises and presence. As I look around me and see all the wonders You have created, I'll shout for joy. I'll revel in wonder. I'll grow tall in Your garden and continue to be productive, even when I'm old. May I be a story reflecting Your glory. In Jesus' name, amen.

A SHADOW AMID THE DARKNESS

Keep awake! Watch at all times. The devil is working against you. He is walking around like a hungry lion with his mouth open. He is looking for someone to eat. Stand against him and be strong in your faith. Remember, other Christians over all the world are suffering the same as you are. After you have suffered for awhile, God Himself will make you perfect. He will keep you in the right way. He will give you strength.
1 PETER 5:8–10 NLV

. . . .

Sometimes, Lord, I forget what I'm up against. That there is a liar, a shadow amid the darkness, a devil working against me. Your description of him walking around like a ravenous lion with his jaw open gnaws at my peace a bit. But then I remember who You are. That with You I can stand against that devil and be strong in my faith. That other Christians around the world are suffering along with me, if not more. Yet still, You are with me, making me perfect, keeping me on the right path, giving me strength, and most of all, filling me with Your abundant peace. Amen.

Day 282

REJOICING ON THE WAY

An angel of the Lord said to Philip, "Rise and go." . . .
And he rose and went. . . . The Spirit said to Philip,
"Go over and join this chariot." So Philip ran to [the eunuch]
. . . . And [Philip] baptized him. And when they came up out
of the water, the Spirit of the Lord carried Philip away, and
the eunuch saw him no more, and went on his way rejoicing.
ACTS 8:26–27, 29–30, 38–39 ESV

. . . .

Lord, I love living in Your Word, experiencing Your joy, growing in my faith. But You want me to do more. You want me to share You with others so that they too can experience all those things, all those blessings from You. So today, Lord, I pray that You would keep me ever attentive to Your direction. That You would open my ears to the voice of Your Spirit. And that once I hear that voice, You would enable me to go where the Spirit wants me to go, do what He wants me to do, and say what He wants me to say so that others can go on Your way rejoicing. In Jesus' name I pray, amen.

Day 283

WALK STEADILY

By faith Enoch was taken up so that he should not see death, and he was not found, because God had taken him. Now before he was taken he was commended as having pleased God. And without faith it is impossible to please him, for whoever would draw near to God must believe that he exists and that he rewards those who seek him.

HEBREWS 11:5–6 ESV

Lord, as I draw near to You today, I have great peace and expectations. For You have said that whoever comes near You needs to believe You are real, not just a remedy for the masses. To me You *are* more real and true than the chair on which I sit, the desk on which I write, the phone on which I talk. And I want to walk with You just as Enoch did so many thousands of years ago. Because he walked steadily with You, Lord, You just took him one day (Genesis 5:21–24). He was simply gone from the earth. What a reward! As I draw near to You today, Lord, show me what I can do to please You. Amen.

Day 284

SMALL BEGINNING, GREATER END

*If you will seek God diligently and make your supplication
to the Almighty, then, if you are pure and upright, surely
He will bestir Himself for you and make your righteous
dwelling prosperous again. And though your beginning
was small, yet your latter end would greatly increase. . . .
Behold, as surely as God will never uphold wrongdoers,
He will never cast away a blameless man. He will yet fill your
mouth with laughter. . .and your lips with joyful shouting.*

JOB 8:5–7, 20–21 AMPC

. . . .

When things seem to be going badly, when nothing seems
to be going my way, Lord, I hang on to the hope that You
will hear and answer my prayer. For Your Son has made
me pure and blameless in Your eyes. Your Son has paved
the way so that when I seek after You and lift my soul to
You, You bend Your ear to my lips. I believe, Lord, that You
will not only move on my behalf but make things better
than they were before—in Your own time. I believe, Lord,
that You will never turn away but will erase my tears.
You, in Your love and compassion, will once again fill my
mouth with laughter and my lips with shouts of joy. In
Jesus' name I pray, amen.

Day 285

EVERY KIND OF PEACE

*She [your sister church here] in Babylon, [who is] elect
(chosen) with [yourselves], sends you greetings, and [so
does] my son (disciple) Mark. Salute one another with
a kiss of love [the symbol of mutual affection]. To all
of you that are in Christ Jesus (the Messiah), may there
be peace (every kind of peace and blessing, especially
peace with God, and freedom from fears, agitating
passions, and moral conflicts). Amen (so be it).*
1 PETER 5:13–14 AMPC

. . . .

That's what I want and need, Lord. Every kind of peace.
For every situation. For every moment I live and breathe.
I want peace within and without. I want peace to grow
up in You. I want peace to fall upon people everywhere
on this earth so that there will be more kindness than
cruelty. So that wars will cease. So that children can go
to school without being afraid. Lord, most of all, I want
peace with You and freedom from fears. No more conflict,
no more tension, no more stress, no more angst. Help me
find every kind of peace, Lord, and then pass it on. In
Jesus' name, amen.

Day 286

THE RIGHT WAY TO JOY

To do what is right and good and fair is more pleasing to the Lord than gifts given on the altar in worship. . . . When what is right and fair is done, it is a joy for those who are right with God. . . . He who follows what is right and loving and kind finds life, right-standing with God and honor. . . . The horse is made ready for war, but winning the fight belongs to the Lord.
PROVERBS 21:3, 15, 21, 31 NLV

. . . .

Lord, sometimes I just don't understand this world. So many people think they hold the right answers, yet those same answers are not of You. They don't seem to jibe with what You would have Your followers be and do. Yet the "right people" who appear to be "wrong in You" seem to be increasing. Justice seems to be the golden ring society rarely obtains. So I'm looking to You, Lord. Help me do what is right, good, and fair in Your eyes. Give me the strength to please You alone, despite the people pleasers who surround me. Help me follow the good way, the right path, *Your* path, leaving the results to You. For only then will I find joy the "right" way. Amen.

EYES ON THE LORD

*Because Moses had faith, he would not be called the
son of Pharaoh's daughter when he grew up. He chose
to suffer with God's people instead of having fun doing
sinful things for awhile. Any shame that he suffered
for Christ was worth more than all the riches in Egypt.
He kept his eyes on the reward God was going to give
him. Because Moses had faith, he left Egypt. He was
not afraid of the king's anger. Moses did not turn from
the right way but kept seeing God in front of him.*

HEBREWS 11:24–27 NLV

Lord, Moses wasn't perfect—and neither am I. That's not
a boast, just a fact. Yet it's a good fact, because Moses'
story proves that even fallible human beings like me can
become great heroes of faith. So here I am, Lord. My eye is
on the reward You have waiting for me. And because You
are with me as I walk down this road of life, I'm rewarded
with the peace I can find only in You, Lord. And because of
Your presence and Your peace, I am not afraid of anyone's
anger or power. All I do is keep my eyes on You, Lord, as
You walk in front of me, going before me, one step, one
day at a time. Amen.

Day 288

FREEDOM IN JOY

Peter was held in prison. But the church kept praying
to God for him. . . . Peter was sleeping between two
soldiers. . . . The angel hit Peter on the side and said,
"Get up!" Then the chains fell off his hands. . . . He went
to Mary's house. . . . Peter knocked at the gate. . . .
In her joy [Rhoda] forgot to open the gate. She ran in
and told them that Peter was standing outside.
ACTS 12:5–7, 12–14 NLV

The joy of answered prayer! The joy in knowing we have access to You. The happiness in the knowledge that we can come to You, give You our heartfelt concerns, and know You have heard us, that You will act on our behalf. The power You exude in response—reaching across time and space, sending down Your angels, and having them work out Your will in Your way as You free us, our family, our friends, and total strangers from the constraints that bind us. Lord, thank You for hearing our prayers. For moving on our behalf. For the answers You provide—ones that defy all expectations and imaginations and leave us overcome with joy. Amen.

Day 289

AT HOME ONCE MORE

The Scripture says, No man who believes in Him [who adheres to, relies on, and trusts in Him] will [ever] be put to shame or be disappointed. [No one] for there is no distinction. . . . The same Lord is Lord over all [of us] and He generously bestows His riches upon all who call upon Him [in faith]. For everyone who calls upon the name of the Lord [invoking Him as Lord] will be saved.
ROMANS 10:11–13 AMPC

. . . .

When I'm down-and-out, fuming and frustrated, alone and abused, concerned and confused, I reach out for You, Lord. In faith, I seek Your presence, Your power, Your touch, Your love, Your strength, Your protection, and Your peace. All seems elusive. My thoughts remain unfocused. And then I remember the power of You, Jesus—the power of Your name. I clear my head and throat and then say, "Jesus. . . Jesus. . .Jesus." At the sound of Your name, my agitation begins to fade. I find my footing, my peace, my Lord. Once more in Your presence, I am whole and at home. In Your name, amen.

Day 290

FROM DAWN TO DUSK

He spread a cloud for a covering, and fire to give light at night. They asked, and He brought them quails for meat. And He filled them with the bread of heaven. He opened the rock and water flowed out. It flowed in the desert like a river. . . . He remembered His holy Word. . . . He brought His people out with joy, His chosen ones with singing.

PSALM 105:39–43 NLV

When I need to hide, Lord, You protect me, covering me with a cloud. When I am walking in darkness, in the deep shadows of night, You provide a fire to give light. When I ask for food, when I thirst for water, You provide both in abundance. You remember Your promises, and You keep Your word. All the ways You take care of me are more than I can fathom, Lord. Be with me once more this day, from the time I begin my work for You until the moment I lay down my head. Bring me through, Lord, with joy. May my last thoughts be songs of praise to You. In Jesus' name, amen.

Day 291

A GOOD LOOK

Do not judge and criticize and condemn others, so that you may not be judged and criticized and condemned yourselves. For just as you judge and criticize and condemn others, you will be judged and criticized and condemned, and in accordance with the measure you [use to] deal out to others, it will be dealt out again to you.

MATTHEW 7:1–2 AMPC

Oftentimes, Lord, You tell me through Your Word that I'll reap what I sow. That whenever I judge and criticize others, I too will be judged and criticized. Help me keep this in mind, Lord, when I come to You complaining that I've lost my peace. For that's when I need to take a good look at myself, to consider when I may have picked on others, pointed out their failures, and picked at their faults. For it may be that that critical spirit with which I attacked others may have just attached itself to me, sucking all the peace out of my life. Help me replace my critical attitude, Lord, with one of encouragement and praise. Help me find and bring out the best in all. In Jesus' name, amen.

Day 292

TWO THINGS. . .

Two things I have asked of You. . . . Take lies and what is
false far from me. Do not let me be poor or rich. Feed me
with the food that I need. Then I will not be afraid that
I will be full and turn my back against You and say,
"Who is the Lord?" And I will not be afraid that I will be
poor and steal, and bring shame on the name of my God.
PROVERBS 30:7–9 NLV

. . . .

Two things that steal joy, Lord: getting caught in a snare
of lies and living in a state of discontentment. So I bring
You this prayer. First, Lord, please give me the courage to
be honest. For all lies are against You, the God of truth.
Second, Lord, please grant me enough to live on—no more,
no less. Not more, because I don't want "stuff"—possessions, treasures on earth—to come between me and You.
Yet not less, so that I won't have to depend on others or
be tempted to take from others and bring disgrace to me
and You. That's it, Lord. The truth and enough to get by.
That will be all I need to gain, maintain, and proclaim my
joy in You! In Jesus' name I pray, amen.

Day 293

STAND AMAZED

The LORD is merciful and gracious, slow to anger and abounding in steadfast love. He will not always chide, nor will he keep his anger forever. He does not deal with us according to our sins, nor repay us according to our iniquities. For as high as the heavens are above the earth, so great is his steadfast love toward those who fear him; as far as the east is from the west, so far does he remove our transgressions from us.
PSALM 103:8–12 ESV

When I think about how much You love me, Lord, I stand amazed at Your patience, tolerance, and compassion. For I am a woman who has at times given in to temptation, entertained a doubt or two, and definitely made mistakes here and there. Yet still I have peace, because Your Word tells me that You, Lord, have an amazing amount of mercy and grace. You are slow to get angry and have loads of love. Even more amazing, Lord, is that You don't deal with me like I deserve. Instead, You have limitless love for me, so much so that You separate me from my mistakes. In You and Your love, I stand amazed. Amen.

Day 294

GOOD THINGS

Some traveled through the desert wastes. They did not find a way. . . . Their souls became weak within them. Then they cried out to the Lord in their trouble. And He took them out of their suffering. He led them by a straight path. . . . He fills the thirsty soul. And He fills the hungry soul with good things. . . . Let them give Him gifts of thanks and tell of His works with songs of joy.
PSALM 107:4–7, 9, 22 NLV

. . . .

So often, Lord, I find myself just wandering. I cannot find my way in, out, over, around, under, or through. And as I go on wandering, my soul grows weak within me. Then I look up. I cry to You, longing to see Your face. And You come quickly. You lift me up, turn me around, show me the right way to go. As I follow Your directions, I see glimpses of You out ahead of me, beckoning, encouraging, loving. And in the resting places, You quench my thirsty and hungering soul with good—all that I need to thrive, to continue on with You. It is for this and so much more that I sing a song of praise and joy to You, the God of my life. Amen.

Day 295

KEEPING ON

Keep on asking and it will be given you; keep on seeking and you will find; keep on knocking [reverently] and [the door] will be opened to you. For everyone who keeps on asking receives; and he who keeps on seeking finds; and to him who keeps on knocking, [the door] will be opened.
MATTHEW 7:7–8 AMPC

. . . .

Lord, I have a feeling I am not as persistent as I could and should be when it comes to prayer requests. It seems I get too easily frustrated and impatient if an answer does not land on my doorstep a day or two after my prayer. Soon disappointment and doubts begin to darken my door and disturb my peace. So it's time to change things up, Lord, to pray as You instruct. From here on, I'm going to ask and keep on asking, seek and keep on seeking, knock and keep on knocking, day after day. And I will do so knowing that I *will* receive what I ask for, *find* what I seek, and see the door *open* that I've been knocking on. Amen.

POWER RELEASED

He, having received [so strict a] charge, put them into the inner prison (the dungeon) and fastened their feet in the stocks. But about midnight, as Paul and Silas were praying and singing hymns of praise to God, and the [other] prisoners were listening to them, suddenly there was a great earthquake, so that the very foundations of the prison were shaken; and at once all the doors were opened and everyone's shackles were unfastened.

ACTS 16:24–26 AMPC

It's true, Lord, that sometimes joy leads me into praising You. But oftentimes, I find that even when joy seems elusive, when I just can't get there from where I am, praise pulls my heart out of the darkness and my mind off its troubles, and brings me right smack into joy! So here I am, Lord, coming to You chained by my sorrow, my mood, my darkness. I'm raising my voice in praise and song to You. And as I do, as my words leave my lips and rise up to Your ears, I find Your power unleashed. The foundation of my troubles, worries, and what-ifs are shaken to their core! And all at once, my door to You—to joy—is opened. I'm free of my shackles! Thank You for releasing me and pulling me into You! Amen!

Day 297

A WISE WOMAN

"Everyone then who hears these words of mine and does them will be like a wise man who built his house on the rock. And the rain fell, and the floods came, and the winds blew and beat on that house, but it did not fall, because it had been founded on the rock. And everyone who hears these words of mine and does not do them will be like a foolish man who built his house on the sand. And the rain fell, and the floods came, and the winds blew and beat against that house, and it fell, and great was the fall of it."
MATTHEW 7:24–27 ESV

Lord, part of my walk with You is about not just *hearing* Your words but *taking some action* to live them. For I want to be a wise woman, to construct my house, my life, on the solid rock of Your Word. When I build on Your foundation, my life won't be toppled by wind and water. Please give me some guidance, Lord, as to what words of Yours I should write on my heart and mind at this moment in time. What wisdom do You have for me to partake of today and forever? Amen.

INTO HIS KEEPING

[The jailer]. . .fell down before Paul and Silas. . . .
Men, what is it necessary for me to do that I may be
saved? And they answered, Believe in the Lord Jesus
Christ [give yourself up to Him, take yourself out of your
own keeping and entrust yourself into His keeping] and
you will be saved, [and this applies both to] you and your
household as well. . . . Then he. . .leaped much for joy.
ACTS 16:29–31, 34 AMPC

So often, Lord, I find that I really haven't given You all of me. I attempt to take care of myself, to trust my own skills, resources, and knowledge. I actually think I know better than You! Today, Jesus, make me a woman totally in Your keeping. Help me give You all of me, to leave nothing behind. To entrust all things to You—my mind, body, soul, spirit, family, friends, country, possessions, present, and future. Remind me of Your power, grace, forgiveness, and wisdom. Help me get it through my head that only by taking myself out of my own keeping and into Yours will I find the joy that will make me want to leap, to dance, to sing in Your name. Amen.

GOD'S PEACE PARAMETERS

*May grace (God's favor) and peace (which is perfect
well-being, all necessary good, all spiritual prosperity,
and freedom from fears and agitating passions and moral
conflicts) be multiplied to you in [the full, personal, precise,
and correct] knowledge of God and of Jesus our Lord.
For His divine power has bestowed upon us all things
that [are requisite and suited] to life and godliness.*
2 PETER 1:2–3 AMPC

. . . .

I am so grateful, Lord, for the peace You have waiting for
me every morning when I awaken, throughout my day, and
into the good night. For Your peace is no ordinary peace.
Your peace is the feeling of perfect well-being, that I have
all the necessary good and all the spiritual prosperity I
could ever dream of or imagine. Your peace is a freedom
from all fears and disturbing passions I might entertain. But
even more wonderful is that Your peace frees me from all
moral conflicts. The fact and promise that this peace will
be multiplied to me is a wonder-filled blessing. No words
can thank You enough, Lord, for pouring Your peace on
me. In Jesus' name, amen.

Day 300

WORD WELCOMED

They answered, Believe in the Lord Jesus Christ. . . .
And they declared the Word of the Lord. . . . And he
took them the same hour of the night and bathed
[them because of their bloody] wounds. . . . Then he
took them up into his house and set food before them;
and he leaped much for joy and exulted with all his
family that he believed in God [accepting and joyously
welcoming what He had made known through Christ].

ACTS 16:31–34 AMPC

. . . .

Oh gentlest of Saviors, how much You still have to teach me.
I *do* believe in You. I put myself entirely in Your keeping,
leaving no remainder behind to fret or fear. And then I
read Your Word, and my eyes are opened. My heart moved.
Your gentleness prompts me to be gentle to others—the
chained, injured, and lost. To pull them close to me and
to tend to their wounds. To share what I have with them.
For as Your Word fills every crevice of want and desire,
I am led to You, Your power, Your grace, Your love, and
Your light, which then flow through me and onto others.
Your Word is more than welcome in my life, Lord. It *is*
my life. Amen.

Day 301

GOD WITH ME

*Look! God's dwelling is with humanity, and He will
live with them. They will be His people, and God
Himself will be with them and be their God. He will
wipe away every tear from their eyes. Death will no
longer exist; grief, crying, and pain will exist no longer,
because the previous things have passed away.*

REVELATION 21:3–4 HCSB

. . . .

Sometimes, Lord, the idea of death frightens me, disturbing
my peace, putting me off balance. Yet then I remember how
things will be in the end. You will be living with us. We will
be Your people, and You will be our God. With Your gentle
hand, You promise to wipe away all tears from our eyes.
Death will no longer be a part of our reality, nor will grief,
crying, and pain. All those things will have passed away,
but we will remain in and with You, our light, our love,
our hope, our Savior. The idea and hope of You awaiting
me at the end of my time on earth restores my peace of
mind and brings a smile to my face. For my joy and peace
are wrapped up in You, my God. Amen.

Day 302

HOME ONCE MORE

Some sat in darkness and in the shadow of death.
They suffered in prison in iron chains. Because they had
turned against the Words of God. . . . Then they cried
out to the Lord in their trouble. And He saved them. . . .
He brought them out of darkness and the shadow of
death. And He broke their chains. . . . Let them give Him
gifts of thanks and tell of His works with songs of joy.
PSALM 107:10–11, 13–14, 22 NLV

. . . .

Even when I go against Your Word, Lord, You save me.
Even when my own stubbornness leads me away from
Your will and toward my own, You hear my cry. When all
around is darkness, You bring me back out into the light
of Your way. You break the ties that have bound me. And
once again, I am humbled. I can barely look up at You. For
although I am full of joy that I am back in Your shadow, I
am full of shame. Why am I so willful? Forgive me, Lord.
Pull me into Your compassionate embrace. Hold me tight
as I snuggle back into Your warmth, so glad to be home
with You once more. Amen.

Day 303

BLESSED WITH PEACE

The voice of the Lord makes the hinds bring forth their young, and His voice strips bare the forests, while in His temple everyone is saying, Glory! The Lord sat as King over the deluge; the Lord [still] sits as King [and] forever! The Lord will give [unyielding and impenetrable] strength to His people; the Lord will bless His people with peace.

PSALM 29:9–11 AMPC

• •

Your voice, Lord, is the power behind all creation. You spoke, and things came into being. You breathed, and I came into being, in Your image, in Your love. Your voice still brings forth young, strips trees, and moves mountains. And as King here, in Your temple, You continue to reign and give strength to Your children. But even more wonderful, Lord, is that You have blessed Your people with peace. Help me to hang on to the ways and wonder of peace. To pass it along when I can. To pray it down upon this land. To cherish it forever and ever in Jesus' name. Amen.

Day 304

ENJOYING THE DAYS

I know that it will be well for those who fear God. . . .
But it will not go well for the sinful. . . . There are right
and good men who have the same thing happen to them
that happens to those who do sinful things. And there
are sinful men who have the same thing happen to them
that happens to those who are right and good. . . . So I
say a man should enjoy himself. . . . Eat and drink and be
happy. . .through the days. . .which God has given him.
ECCLESIASTES 8:12–15 NLV

. . . .

I keep waiting, Lord, for bad people to "get theirs." But they never seem to! And Your Word says that's just how it is. Sometimes bad things happen to good people, and good things happen to bad people. At least on earth, anyway. So help me, Lord, to turn all these thoughts over to You. To realize I'll never be able to figure everything out. But You have, and will, take care of it. Meanwhile, I'm going to enjoy my days with You, right here, right now. I'm going to live and be joy-filled in Your name, amen!

Day 305

MY HOPE

Let us hold unswervingly to the hope we profess, for he who promised is faithful.
HEBREWS 10:23 NIV

. . . .

God, today I'm soul weary and in need of hope. I confess I feel anxious about my current circumstances and desperately need You to fill me from the inside out. When I focus on what's lacking, I feel heavy inside; and as much as I don't want to feel this way, I do.

Thank You for loving me just as I am. Forgive me for focusing on my circumstances, which shift like the weather. Invite me to cling to You. My steadfast, unwavering hope is found in You alone. Whether in plenty or want, my heart desperately wants You to lighten the weight inside and fill me with expectancy of Your spirit. Where anxiety threatens, I'm asking for You to stir me to pray aloud, *God, be my hope.* In Jesus' name I pray, amen.

Day 306

HEAVENLY DEW

You will guard him and keep him in perfect and constant peace whose mind [both its inclination and its character] is stayed on You, because he commits himself to You, leans on You, and hopes confidently in You. So trust in the Lord (commit yourself to Him, lean on Him, hope confidently in Him) forever. . . . You who dwell in the dust, awake and sing for joy! For Your dew [O Lord] is a dew of [sparkling] light [heavenly, supernatural dew].
ISAIAH 26:3–4, 19 AMPC

. . . .

I'm keeping my mind, heart, soul, and spirit focused on You, Lord. For when I do, Your guard of peace comes up all around me. Its shield keeps me still within, no matter what is happening without. In You I find my refuge, for to You alone I am committed. On You alone I lean. All my hope and expectation lie in You—not just today, in this moment on earth, but forever. Beyond this day and all the days to come. Rain down Your love upon me, Lord. For it's Your refreshment that keeps me from running dry and in the current of Your presence and all the love and joy that come with it. Amen.

A PRAYER FOR A HURTING HEART

He has made everything beautiful in its time. Also, he has
put eternity into man's heart, yet so that he cannot find
out what God has done from the beginning to the end.
ECCLESIASTES 3:11 ESV

. . . .

God, my heart is hurt. There are people I feel unseen and misunderstood by. Legitimate, real hurts, and I can't flip a switch and suddenly forgive. Please assure me that You see my hurting heart and understand my pain. You appreciate my honesty and don't want me to cover up my true feelings. Even in my inability to forgive, please make my heart a little more tender and moldable than yesterday.

Can You please remind me how You see me today so that I can claim Your promises and take one small step toward ultimate forgiveness? Thank You for Your patience with my process. I trust You are making all things beautiful in Your time. Soften my heart even as I work and walk and tune my ear to Your Word. Amen.

Day 308

EAGERLY AWAITING

I bore you on eagles' wings and brought you to Myself. . . .The eternal God is your refuge and dwelling place, and underneath are the everlasting arms. . . . [Looking forward to the shepherd's arrival, the eager girl pictures their meeting and says]. . . Oh, that his left hand were under my head and that his right hand embraced me! . . . Let all those that seek and require You rejoice and be glad in You.

EXODUS 19:4; DEUTERONOMY 33:27;
SONG OF SOLOMON 8:1, 3; PSALM 40:16 AMPC

Lord, thank You for hovering over me. For bearing me on eagles' wings, bringing me out of myself and into You. You are my refuge. In You I live, move, and have my being. You hold me up when I'm down. You turn my life around. Each and every morning, I look for You, eagerly anticipating the calm, peace, love, and joy I'll experience when Your left hand gently cradles my head and Your right hand draws me into You. Come, Lord. I'm waiting. I'm willing and ready to melt into Your love and affection. In Jesus' name I pray, amen.

KINGDOM PERSPECTIVE

He told them another parable: "The kingdom of heaven is like a mustard seed, which a man took and planted in his field. Though it is the smallest of all seeds, yet when it grows, it is the largest of garden plants and becomes a tree, so that the birds come and perch in its branches."
MATTHEW 13:31–32 NIV

God, You say the kingdom is like a mustard seed, and mustard seeds are small. How often do I think of the word *kingdom* and imagine big, flashy, and powerful? To You, kingdom perspective is about the heart. Forgive me for getting caught up in the world's perspective of kingdom instead of Your eternal kingdom. Stir me toward grand in Your eyes—small as a mustard seed. This is my goal.

Whisper Your delight in me as I go about the small tasks of my day. Please remind me that these mustard seed miracles are building "the largest of plants" where shade and refuge will be available to others. I desire to have a heart that follows Your lead, regardless of outcome or status. Your kingdom is coming, and what matters most is my eternal deposits I'm making on earth: You and people. This is enough. Amen.

Day 310

A JOYFUL WALK WITH JESUS

I am going. . .bound by the [Holy] Spirit and
obligated and compelled by the [convictions of my own]
spirit, not knowing what will befall me. . .except that
the Holy Spirit clearly and emphatically affirms to me. . .
that imprisonment and suffering await me. But none
of these things move me; neither do I esteem my life
dear to myself, if only I may finish my course with
joy and the ministry which I have obtained from
[which was entrusted to me by] the Lord Jesus.
ACTS 20:22–24 AMPC

I'm not really sure what lies before me, Lord. Only You can see all things that have been, are, and will be. But I know that Your Spirit is leading my spirit, urging me to move ahead, to continue on with the gifts You have given me, in the direction You have sent me. Whatever happens, good or bad, doesn't really matter to me. The only desire I have is to finish my walk with You with joy, working where and when You allow. Thank You, Lord, for making me a part of Your plan. In Jesus' name I pray, amen.

Day 311

A RHYTHM OF DEPENDENCE

> *The heart of man plans his way,*
> *but the LORD establishes his steps.*
> PROVERBS 16:9 ESV

. . . .

Like the familiar hymn, Lord, *I need You, oh, I need You, every hour I need You.*

God, I desperately want to depend on You and acknowledge how much easier it is for me to kick into self-dependence. Forgive me for relying on myself, my strength, my pep-talk spirit. I confess I am weary and don't want to go another minute on my own. Help me, even as I struggle to understand what it means to fully depend on You. Help me pay attention when I release control and when I greedily take charge.

Awaken me to what dependence looks like with You, so that I may create a rhythm of laying myself aside in order that You may lead. And as I do, God, please help me feel lighter inside, in ways only Your Spirit can. This is my heart's cry. Amen.

HEALING WORD

Some were fools because of their wrong-doing.
They had troubles because of their sins. . . . And they
came near the gates of death. Then they cried out to
the Lord in their trouble. And He saved them from their
suffering. He sent His Word and healed them. And He
saved them from the grave. . . . Let them give Him gifts
of thanks and tell of His works with songs of joy.
PSALM 107:17–20, 22 NLV

Whenever I miss the target You've set for me, Lord, trouble follows. Only then, it seems, do I stop and regret the things I said or did. Only then do I cry out for You to save me from the consequences of my sin. And even then, the times when I'm not proud of myself in any way, shape, or form, You come when I call. You save me, pull me out, lift me up, restore me. You send Your Word to heal me. You give me life once more. There is no way I can ever repay all You do for me, Lord. All I can offer is my humble thanks and songs of joy, love, and gratitude. Amen.

Day 313

PATIENT PERSEVERANCE

The Lord is my shepherd; I shall not want. He makes me lie down in green pastures. He leads me beside still waters. He restores my soul. He leads me in paths of righteousness for his name's sake.
Psalm 23:1–3 esv

God, I'm laughing because You know me and my urgency to move quickly, to activate, to check off boxes and focus on the next task. Still me, Lord. Please shift my activator mindset toward patient perseverance—slow and steady. A steadfast tenacity to keep going despite difficulty in seeing success or an outcome. This is faith. This is trust.

Rest my soul. I breathe deep of Your love. Your time frame is contingent, not on success, but on matters of the soul. You are not worried about my achievements but care mostly about equipping me with strength for the journey. Patient perseverance is my prayer. I ask confidently and know You are restoring my steps for today. Amen.

Day 314

OPEN TO JOY

Give strength to weak hands and to weak knees. Say to those whose heart is afraid, "Have strength of heart, and do not be afraid. See, your God will come. . . . He will save you." Then the eyes of the blind will be opened. And the ears of those who cannot hear will be opened. Then those who cannot walk will jump like a deer. And the tongue of those who cannot speak will call out for joy.
ISAIAH 35:3–6 NLV

Your Word, Lord—oh, how it feeds every part of me! It gives strength, power, and energy to my weak hands and knees. Your Word swells my heart, filling it with the courage I need to face things I'd rather not face, things I can overcome only when You stand with me. Your Word opens the eyes of my heart each time I look within its pages. Your voice reveals new meanings, helping me to understand things that were once cloudy. You make me want to leap and shout for joy! Continue with me, Lord. Today reveal the wonder and power of Your Word until my soul once again rejoices. Amen.

ACTIVE LISTENING

"These things I have spoken to you while I am still with you. But the Helper, the Holy Spirit, whom the Father will send in my name, he will teach you all things and bring to your remembrance all that I have said to you."

JOHN 14:25–26 ESV

. . . .

God, help me listen to Your voice more than anyone else's. With all the voices and noise and buzz on social media, in our communities, and even in my home, I can easily forget pausing, being still, and actively listening to You.

God, I'm sorry for being quick to offer my ears to what is urgent and reactive, rather than responsive and slow. Your words come in the quiet, in the everyday, and I long to still myself to listen—*really* listen—and then actively respond and step obediently into where You are calling me. Forgive me for listening to others first. For creating idols in well-intentioned relationships before filtering my heart with You first.

I quiet myself before You. I'm here. Expectantly listening to Your voice. Amen.

Day 316

GIVING FIRST TO GOD

*[The Macedonian churches] have been put to the test
by much trouble, but they have much joy. They have
given much even though they were very poor.
They gave as much as they could because they wanted
to. They asked from their hearts if they could help the
Christians in Jerusalem. It was more than we expected.
They gave themselves to the Lord first. Then they gave
themselves to us to be used as the Lord wanted.*

2 CORINTHIANS 8:2–5 NLV

. . . .

There is such joy in giving, Lord. But there are so many
worthy causes. It can be difficult to know which to choose.
So, Lord, make Your desires clear to me. As I give myself
first to You, I'm relying on You to help me to home in on
the causes You want me to support through service, provisions, or money. Lord, I want to give from the heart and
soul. And after I do, I'm not going to worry about where
my next dollar will be coming from but will rely on You to
provide for me as I help provide for others—with absolute
joy and pleasure. In Jesus' name, amen.

DELIGHTFUL CELEBRATION

Rejoice in the Lord always. I will say it again: Rejoice!
Let your gentleness be evident to all. The Lord is
near. Do not be anxious about anything, but in every
situation, by prayer and petition, with thanksgiving,
present your requests to God. And the peace of God,
which transcends all understanding, will guard
your hearts and your minds in Christ Jesus.
PHILIPPIANS 4:4–7 NIV

God, I find it easy to celebrate when life is going as planned, when circumstances are favorable and comfortable. Yet, I know You do Your greatest work in my discomfort. But for today, I will rejoice. I will tuck this moment away and pull it out for the hard days.

As Job said, we are so quick to praise in the good and complain in the hard. Forgive me, God, for treating You like a genie and questioning Your ways when life goes off course. Today, I will pull out the fancy china, sing in the car, and smile at every stranger. I will celebrate, for I am savoring every moment, every feeling, every creation sighting and conversation. You are in all of this, and to You I give thanks and experience sheer and utter delight! Amen.

Day 318

A JOYFUL COMEBACK

"Come back to me and really mean it!" . . . Change your
life, not just your clothes. Come back to GOD, your God.
And here's why: God is kind and merciful. He takes a
deep breath, puts up with a lot, this most patient God,
extravagant in love, always ready to cancel catastrophe.
Who knows? Maybe he'll do it now, maybe he'll turn
around and show pity. Maybe, when all's said and done,
there'll be blessings full and robust for your GOD!
JOEL 2:12–14 MSG

Lord, I know sometimes I'm just not there for You. Not like You're always here for me. I've gotten so busy living life, I've forgotten to live it for You! As a result, all joy seems to have gone out of me. So forgive me, God, for wandering away. I know You are kind, loving, and compassionate. You have so much more love for me than I do for myself right now, Lord. So let's change things up. As I come back to You, Lord, come back to me. Turn my life around to the good. Shower Your blessings upon me as I joyfully await Your power and presence in my life once more! In Jesus' name, amen.

Day 319

A DEEP BREATH OF GRACE

For by grace you have been saved through faith.
And this is not your own doing; it is the gift of God,
not a result of works, so that no one may boast.
EPHESIANS 2:8–9 ESV

. . . .

God, I'm noticing that my grace well is dry. I'm cranky and selfish, and life seems half empty. Thank You for loving me as I am, but I know You desire more; You long for me to believe You saved me by Your grace, and because of this, I can fully offer grace to those around me. Offer me a deep breath of grace right now. I don't have to work for Your love—I'm covered. May this knowledge sink into my bones.

God, I want to be a soul who lavishes grace because I know of my need for Your grace first. Soak my soul in the gift of knowing You. As I spend time with You, may grace naturally overflow. A grace giver is who I want to be. Forgive me for expecting this gift when I'm quick to expect others to earn their favor from me. Grace upon grace upon grace is my prayer. Amen.

Day 320

FREEDOM TO CHOOSE

*You were chosen to be free. Be careful that you do not
please your old selves by sinning because you are free.
Live this free life by loving and helping others. . . .
Let the Holy Spirit lead you in each step. Then you will
not please your sinful old selves. . . . The fruit that comes
from having the Holy Spirit in our lives is: love, joy,
peace, not giving up, being kind, being good, having faith,
being gentle, and being the boss over our own desires.*

GALATIANS 5:13, 16, 22–23 NLV

. . . .

Your Word, Lord, makes it clear that You *chose* me to be
free! For that privilege I praise You, Lord. Yet I don't want
that same freedom to lead me to please myself. I want
to please *You.* And the only way to do that is by letting
Your Holy Spirit lead me every way, every day. So help
me, Lord, to keep close to You. To home in on what the
Holy Spirit would have me to do, where He would have
me go. Then I will have the love, joy, peace, and so much
more that comes from walking in Your will and way! In
Jesus' name I pray, amen.

Day 321

STRENGTH IN WEAKNESS

*But he said to me, "My grace is sufficient for you,
for my power is made perfect in weakness." Therefore
I will boast all the more gladly of my weaknesses,
so that the power of Christ may rest upon me.*
2 CORINTHIANS 12:9 ESV

God, please forgive me. I am heaping shame on myself for not being tougher, for being too emotional. This is not of You. You made me with emotions. You don't expect me to stuff them down or pep talk them away.

Please use my weakness, the areas I feel most dependent and needy, to find my need in You. Forgive me for trying to be tough and positive on my own. Forgive me for harsh self-talk. Please tender me with a sensitive spirit to find my strength in Your "enoughness."

God, You say that when I am weakest, Your power is the strongest. I need Your strength to fill in my weak spaces. I offer my brokenness, my weariness, my weakness, and I trust You are doing a beautiful work of renewing strength void of anything I can do on my own. Please rest Your power upon me, God. I will walk under Your strong covering just as I am, weakness and all. Amen.

Day 322

REGAINING STRENGTH

Let them give Him gifts of thanks and tell of His works
with songs of joy. Some went out to sea in ships. . . .
He spoke and raised up a storm. . . . Their strength of
heart left them in their danger. . . . They did not know
what to do. Then they cried out to the Lord in their
trouble. And He took them out of all their problems.
He stopped the storm, and the waves of the sea became
quiet. Then they were glad because the sea became
quiet. And He led them to the safe place they wanted.
PSALM 107:22–23, 25–30 NLV

. . . .

When I go out on my own, I usually end up exhausted,
just when I need the most strength. That's when I finally
realize I've left You out of my boat, Lord. I cry to You,
and You come to my rescue. You stop the wind and the
waves. In the quiet, I hear Your voice. I'm overwhelmed
with gladness. My heart regains strength. And You lead me
to the exact place I'd been heading all along. Thank You,
Lord, for always being there for me, helping me, rescuing
me, delivering me. Amen.

Day 323

A CHANGE IN THE WEATHER

*"While the earth remains, seedtime and
harvest, cold and heat, summer and winter,
day and night, shall not cease."*
GENESIS 8:22 ESV

. . . .

God, the weather is changing. And as it does, would You turn my soul with it? Toward a new way of seeing You? My neighborhood? This community? There's beauty in shifting seasons, for they invite our hearts into a fresh mindset.

Please give me courage to lay down habits and relationships that are heavy and toxic. I'm following You and will continue stepping into this next season with an openness to how You are leading, revealing, and making all things new.

Forgive me for standing stubbornly in security and comfort. I open my hands and heart to You now, even as the temperature and weather changes. Please invite me deeper into Your heart and give me strength to release what I no longer need to grasp tightly to so that I may free myself to cling to You. Please use this change in weather to uncover a deeper awareness of You. Amen.

THIRSTING FOR GOD'S VOICE

*Wait and listen, everyone who is thirsty! Come to the
waters; and he who has no money, come, buy and eat!
Yes, come, buy [priceless, spiritual] wine and milk
without money and without price [simply for the self-
surrender that accepts the blessing]. Why do you spend
your money for that which is not bread, and your
earnings for what does not satisfy? Hearken diligently
to Me, and eat what is good, and let your soul delight
itself in fatness [the profuseness of spiritual joy].*
ISAIAH 55:1–2 AMPC

. . . .

Lord, I am so ready to drink from Your well of wisdom.
There are so many voices out there, telling me what is
right and what is wrong, what I should do and what I
shouldn't do. Help me, Lord, to silence the words—written
and spoken—of others that are ringing through my head.
Give me the power and strength to focus on Yours alone.
What You have within Your Book is the wisdom I crave.
Show me what You would have me read. Then open the
doors of my mind so that I can comprehend what You're
telling me. Give my soul the joy and delight of Your direction! In Jesus' name I pray, amen.

Day 325

EAGER TO EXPERIENCE

"For the ear tests words as the palate tastes food."
JOB 34:3 ESV

. . . .

God, I wake eager to experience You in the tiny details of today. Before I get out of bed, would You please clear my mind of clutter and distractions so that I can approach the day open and ready to listen. As I go about work, cleaning, and everyday tasks, would You help me notice how Your Spirit meets me in my senses?

Where am I hearing You? What are You saying? What smells evoke memories of when I'm most alive? What tangible things do I touch that turn a grateful heart to You? What am I reading, and is it truth-honoring? Are the foods I eat out of coping or nourishment?

Please help me notice the personal ways You woo me and meet me right where I am: at the grocery store, talking with a coworker, and preparing dinner. I often neglect to say yes to Your all-sensory invitations knocking at every turn. Still my heart to notice, and may I answer with anticipation and a gladness of spirit. Amen.

Day 326

ROOTS IN REALITY

Every time you cross my mind, I break out in exclamations
of thanks to God. Each exclamation is a trigger to prayer.
I find myself praying for you with a glad heart. . . .
There has never been the slightest doubt in my mind
that the God who started this great work in you would
keep at it and bring it to a flourishing finish. . . .
It's not at all fanciful for me to think this way about
you. My prayers and hopes have deep roots in reality.
PHILIPPIANS 1:3–4, 6–7 MSG

So many "things" go through my mind in one day, one hour, one moment, one second, Lord. And sometimes I never stop to dwell on any of them. I just keep focused on the task before me. Yet in doing that, Lord, I can miss Your prompts to pray for someone. So, Lord, help me break out in joyful recognition when someone crosses my mind. Allow that face or name to trigger a prayer on his or her behalf. May I pray that whatever You've begun in that individual will flourish. For prayers aren't just empty incantations—they change reality! In Jesus' name, amen!

Day 327

BEAUTY ALL AROUND

*The heavens declare the glory of God; the skies proclaim
the work of his hands. . . . Their voice goes out into
all the earth, their words to the ends of the world.
In the heavens God has pitched a tent for the sun. . . .
It rises at one end of the heavens and makes its circuit
to the other; nothing is deprived of its warmth.*

PSALM 19:1, 4, 6 NIV

Lord, I feel the need for beauty deep down in my bones.
I need a hint of eternity, of rainbow sunsets, of butterflies
and vibrant fields, of pure, raw beauty. How easy it is to go
about my day and overlook Your beauty invitations: in the
faces of my kids, the hug of my spouse, the playfulness of
our puppy, the blooming flowers, the colorful skies, and even
the designs on my shirt and the fun texture of my boots.

Forgive me, God, when I bypass beauty. Please invite
me to pause and look up and around and down. Help me
see beauty in Your people.

Where is beauty today? God, I'm on a mission to notice
and reflect and to invite others to do the same. Amen.

MIND EXCHANGE

Incline your ear [submit and consent to the divine will] and come to Me; hear, and your soul will revive. . . . Seek, inquire for, and require the Lord while He may be found [claiming Him by necessity and by right]; call upon Him while He is near. . . . For My thoughts are not your thoughts, neither are your ways My ways, says the Lord. . . . You shall go out. . .with joy and be led forth [by your Leader, the Lord Himself, and His word] with peace.

Isaiah 55:3, 6, 8, 12 AMPC

. . . .

Help me to readjust my ears so that I can pick up on Your wavelength, Lord. I'm drawing near to You, waiting and wanting to hear what You have to say. Refresh my soul, Lord, with Your Word as I seek Your face while You're so near to me. I'm calling out to You, emptying my own mind of its constant dialogue so that I can actually *hear* Your voice and exchange my thoughts for Yours, which are always so far above me yet penetrate deep into my own heart. For when I tap into Your wisdom and love, I find myself tasting Your joy and being led, not just by Your peace but by You Yourself! Amen.

Day 329

SOURCE OF ALL LOVE

Whoever does not love does not know
God, because God is love.
1 JOHN 4:8 NIV

. . . .

You are the source of all love. Anything that reflects love, is in love, or creates love is Yours, God. Love is fullness of light and wonder and beauty. In You there is no darkness or heaviness or shame.

Where do I see love in me? Where am I living through Your love and living loved as a result? Where am I carrying darkness that isn't mine to carry? Forgive me for paying more attention to the existence of darkness, rather than walking confidently in the light.

Lord, my heart cry is this: Where and how can I step fully into Your love today? Where do I resist Your love? Why? Where do I have a hard time allowing all of me to be loved? What's this about? Where do I readily receive Your love? May I bask in the light of Your love and not feel pressure to do anything with it other than humbly receive. Amen.

Day 330

HAPPY IN FAITH

Because of your prayers and the help the Holy Spirit gives me, all of this will turn out for good. . . . To me, living means having Christ. To die means that I would have more of Him. If I keep on living here in this body, it means that I can lead more people to Christ. . . . I have a desire to leave this world to be with Christ, which is much better. But it is more important for you that I stay. I am sure I will live to help you grow and be happy in your faith.

PHILIPPIANS 1:19, 21–25 NLV

Some days, Lord, life can be so hard that I just want You to beam me up. To lift up every part of me into heaven with You. Yet I know You have plans for me that are for my good and Your purpose. So help me to be happy wherever I am, Lord, in heaven or on earth. Remind me that things will, in the end, always turn out for good. Show me, Lord, whom You would have me help and whom You would have me lead to You so they can find joy in You. I live to serve You, Lord. In Jesus' name, amen.

Day 331

SEEKING LOVELY

For by him all things were created, in heaven and on earth, visible and invisible, whether thrones or dominions or rulers or authorities—all things were created through him and for him. And he is before all things, and in him all things hold together.
COLOSSIANS 1:16–17 ESV

Lovely is what I'm seeking today. Lovely in spirit, in nature, in conversation, in You. Where are You drawing me to notice Your loveliness at home, in the sky, at work? A creative project? When working out? Is Your loveliness in gardening or reading or playing with my kids? Perhaps it's in designing a space or teaching or mowing the lawn.

Your loveliness, Lord, is it also in my broken places? In my pain and hurt and doubts and fears? Help me find Your loveliness in these places as well. Forgive me for closing the door on my ugly spaces and only looking for pretty. Pretty does not equal lovely. Lovely is what You are doing in all things—beautiful and messy. Lovely is the process of reflecting You. Please remind me of this when I'm quick to cover my ugly. Help me see all places objectively, as You see them—lovely to the core. Amen.

THAT MIDDLE GROUND

*If any person thinks himself to be somebody [too
important to condescend to shoulder another's load]
when he is nobody [of superiority except in his own
estimation], he deceives and deludes and cheats himself.
But let every person carefully scrutinize and examine
and test his own conduct and his own work. He can
then have the personal satisfaction and joy of doing
something commendable [in itself alone] without
[resorting to] boastful comparison with his neighbor.*

GALATIANS 6:3–4 AMPC

Lord, too often I find myself comparing my work with that
of others. And then I find myself in one of two places:
I'm either not satisfied or too satisfied with what I've
accomplished. If it's the former, I begin to feel less worthy,
less able, less competent. In other words, I feel less than
who You've made me to be. If it's the latter, I find myself
feeling too worthy, too capable, and too self-sufficient.
Then before I know it, pride has set in. Help me, Lord,
to find that middle ground. To know that my joy lies in
comparing myself with myself and in doing my work for
and in You. That is my reward. In Jesus' name, amen.

Day 333

INTENTIONAL PURPOSE

The plans of the diligent lead surely to abundance,
but everyone who is hasty comes only to poverty.
PROVERBS 21:5 ESV

. . . .

I'm a busy soul. I leave no margin for rest or breathing room on either side of my full calendar. Forgive me, God, for I feel in my body that this is not healthy. When I'm late I become crabby and resentful and angry. I am mad at. . . ? Who? Only I am in charge of my schedule! Here lies my challenge. I'm planning too much and frustrated when I'm exhausted come the end of the day.

Where are You inviting me to plan and live and create intentional space to breathe? Where am I scheduling time to be in Your presence? Am I blowing up the box I have You in and living open to how You breathe life into everyday, mundane tasks? In the cleaning and errands and driving, You are here.

Please help me not to waste another moment rushing frantic from one task to the next, but to live with intentional purpose and mindful awareness that You are with me in all parts of my day. Amen.

SPROUTING WITH HOPE

*He changes a desert into a pool of water and makes water
flow out of dry ground. And He makes the hungry go
there. . . . They plant seeds in the fields and plant grape-
vines and gather much fruit. He lets good come to them
and they become many in number. . . . He lifts those in
need out of their troubles. He makes their families grow
like flocks. Those who are right see it and are glad.*

PSALM 107:35–38, 41–42 NLV

. . . .

When I'm in a place that seems dry of hope, Lord, I pray to
You, and You make water appear out of nowhere. Soon that
once-barren landscape within begins to come back to life.
You open my eyes to what may be. You urge me to plant
seeds of confidence and expectation in You. And soon I'm
bearing more fruit than I ever hoped or imagined. Good
things begin to sprout up, feeding every part of me—mind,
body, spirit, and soul. Once again, Lord, You lift me up out
of myself and into You. And I am overcome with gladness,
singing with joy. Thank You, Lord, for bringing me back to
where You want me to be—joyfully expectant in You. Amen.

Day 335

THIS PAUSE

I believe that I shall look upon the goodness of the Lord in the land of the living! Wait for the Lord; be strong, and let your heart take courage; wait for the Lord!
PSALM 27:13–14 ESV

God, I feel like life is on pause. There's little movement or direction. I'm listening but unsure of how to move forward, or what to lean into. What happens in this pause? Fear. Anxiety. I can feel my blood pressure skyrocket and am tempted to kick into "go mode" simply to make any type of action occur.

Why do I do this? What scares me about being on pause? Please forgive me, Lord, for my impatience. What are You inviting me to notice, learn, or surrender in this in-between place? Where are You asking me to stay when I really just want to crawl out of my skin and make something happen?

Perhaps, Lord, the purpose of this pause isn't the next step but a greater intimacy with knowing You are here. You are in the middle of the "not-yet." You are in control of this pause, and for this reason alone I trust You. Amen.

Day 336

THE WE TRAIN

Are you strong because you belong to Christ?
Does His love comfort you? Do you have joy by
being as one in sharing the Holy Spirit? Do you have
loving-kindness and pity for each other? Then give
me true joy by thinking the same thoughts. Keep having
the same love. Be as one in thoughts and actions. . . .
Think of other people as more important than yourself.
PHILIPPIANS 2:1–3 NLV

Lord, I'm back on that all-about-me train. How do I keep getting stuck here? It never leads to happiness, that's for sure. Help me, Lord, to realize that my strength lies is putting others before myself and finding that my joy is tied up with *their* joy. So lead me today, Lord, to be more others- than self-focused. To keep my eyes open to where I can lend a hand or to whom I can lend an ear. Show me to whom You would have me extend a hand of friendship or a word of love. Instead of finding where I am different from another, show me where she and I are the same and can find common ground. Help me get on the we-train and embark upon a joy-meets-joy journey. In Jesus' name I pray, amen.

Day 337

STILL GOOD

Lord, by such things people live; and my spirit finds
life in them too. You restored me to health and let me
live. Surely it was for my benefit that I suffered such
anguish. In your love you kept me from the pit of
destruction; you have put all my sins behind your back.
ISAIAH 38:16–17 NIV

. . . .

I've been thinking lately about healing. About how we, as believers, pray for healing. What about the times when healing isn't on this side of heaven? Is that still *healing*? What is *true* healing? God, I confess I selfishly pray for people to be healed. For suffering to end. For illnesses to disappear. For cancer to be erased. Why do horrible diseases and tragedies happen? Where are You in these circumstances?

I bring these honest questions to You and trust You can handle them. Know my heart, Lord, and please draw me to find security in You alone. God, perhaps my prayer for healing is an invitation to find my longings fulfilled in eternity with You. Where there is no sickness. Until then, please give me boldness to pray and trust that You heal in out-of-the-box ways. I don't always have to understand to know that You are still good. Amen.

POWER OF THE WORD

The rain and snow come down from heaven and do not return there without giving water to the earth. This makes plants grow on the earth, and gives seeds to the planter and bread to the eater. So My Word which goes from My mouth will not return to Me empty. It will do what I want it to do, and will carry out My plan well. You will go out with joy, and be led out in peace.
ISAIAH 55:10–12 NLV

. . . .

The power of Your Word, Lord, is astounding. Just as the rain and snow You send to earth promote growth to the fields and food to the farmer, so does Your Word provide growth and sustenance in my life. It is food for my soul and water for my spirit. Your Word carries out Your plan for me and all Your children. Your promises, so much stronger than my good intentions, grow me into the person You want and *need* me to be so that Your will on earth will be done. In and because of all this, I am on the path of Your joy, led by Your peace. In Jesus' name, amen!

Day 339

TIME INVESTMENT

*Look carefully then how you walk, not as unwise
but as wise, making the best use of the time, because
the days are evil. Therefore do not be foolish,
but understand what the will of the Lord is.*
EPHESIANS 5:15–17 ESV

. . . .

Much of my day seems governed by time. I watch the clock
hands and feel a familiar twinge of rush. There seems
to be an inner alarm clock threatening to go off when I
entertain the idea of pausing. Forgive me for living on the
edge of exhaustion.

God, I admit, the clock is my idol. I allow it to boss me
around and steal my joy. Could it be, when I offer You my
firsts, that You will maximize my hours? How will You set
the time and give me what I need for today?

Please speak to me about where to invest my minutes
and hours. I want to be in constant communication with
You. Should I say yes to this? What about this? What will
bring You the most glory? What can wait? . . .

I offer my time to You. Please help me steward the
minutes and hours wisely. Amen.

Day 340

CHANGE OF PLANS

Do not always be thinking about your own plans only.
Be happy to know what other people are doing.
Think as Christ Jesus thought. Jesus has always been
as God is. But He did not hold to His rights as God.
He put aside everything that belonged to Him and
made Himself the same as a servant who is owned
by someone. . . . He gave up His important place.
PHILIPPIANS 2:4–8 NLV

Sometimes, Lord, I tend to get so wrapped up in my own life and plans that I never look around or show any interest in what's happening in the lives of others. Help me to reach out, Lord. I actually want to listen to the plans, dreams, and callings in the lives of others. Help me to put aside what I'd planned for today, even if it's just for a little while, and show an interest in another's ideas. And especially help me, Lord, to be more gracious amid interruptions, recognizing them not as something keeping me from getting what *I* want done that day but as opportunities to do what *You* would have me do to serve You. In Jesus' name, amen.

Day 341

EVEN AS I WALK

Dear friend, I pray that you may enjoy good
health and that all may go well with you,
even as your soul is getting along well.
3 JOHN 1:2 NIV

. . . .

God, as I walk up and down our street and notice the clouds and the birds and the flowers that are blooming and grass that is growing, may all of this be a whisper of Your creation. May I not pass by without noticing where You are seeding, uprooting, and showing Yourself in nature. God, thank You for the very legs that I walk on and my health. Forgive me for how easily I take this for granted. Even as I walk, would You strengthen my steps?

Continue to invite me forward to where You are growing me and tethering me deeper to Your Spirit and making me more discerning of Your voice. Thank You that You are a God who walks with, beside, behind, and in front of me. Thank You for hemming me in and companioning me right now, even as I walk. Amen.

Day 342

SHORE OF GOD'S DESIRE

When they had rowed three or four miles, they saw Jesus walking on the sea and approaching the boat. And they were afraid (terrified). But Jesus said to them, It is I; be not afraid! [I Am; stop being frightened!] Then they were quite willing and glad for Him to come into the boat. And now the boat went at once to the land they had steered toward. [And immediately they reached the shore toward which they had been slowly making their way.]

JOHN 6:19–21 AMPC

. . . .

I thank You, Jesus, for always watching out for me. For coming into my life with all Your supernatural strength, with the power You wield to calm the wind and waves that threaten me, within and without. Help me to see You more clearly, Jesus. To recognize You as the friend and water-walker You are. And even more, Lord, make me not just *willing* but *glad* to let You into my boat. For when I do, I know I will be heading the way You want me to go, taking the course Father God planned for me to take. And I will at last find myself reaching the shore of Your desire for me. In Your name I pray, amen.

Day 343

CLOUD-WATCHING

*"Do you know how God controls the clouds
and makes his lightning flash? Do you know
how the clouds hang poised, those wonders
of him who has perfect knowledge?"*

JOB 37:15–16 NIV

. . . .

God, I'm sitting on the porch, staring out at the horizon, mesmerized by the deep blue sky—like a canvas You're eagerly painting. I imagine You sit back, then dab to create a cloud wisp; with Your brush, a rainbow appears.

You offer up sunrises and sunsets and rainbows and rain, and all of this pleases You. God, I love Your creativity. How can I echo this in my day? How can I bring beauty to conversations and work spaces and even my wardrobe? How can I add color and brush moments with kindness? How can I take the peace of cloud-watching into my whole day?

God, even in my desire to embrace the beauty You make, please help me so that I don't feel like I have to mimic, but simply appreciate, Your works. Let me sit in awe of how You design; let me turn my face upward toward the clouds and smile. Amen.

Day 344

JOYFUL AND OBEDIENT

You must keep on working to show you have been saved
from the punishment of sin. Be afraid that you may
not please God. He is working in you. God is helping
you obey Him. God is doing what He wants done in
you. Be glad you can do the things you should be doing.
Do all things without arguing and talking about how
you wish you did not have to do them. In that way,
you can prove yourselves to be without blame.

PHILIPPIANS 2:12–15 NLV

Some days I feel like one of the wandering Israelites, Lord.
I'm moaning and groaning about all the things I don't want
to do. Help me to look at all the blessings in my life instead
of at all the seeming curses. For I want to please You, Lord.
And no one likes a whiner. Open my eyes to what You are
doing within me. Help me not to give up on myself—or
You—but recognize that You are helping me follow the
path You have purposefully put before me. Make me not
stubborn but pliant to Your directions. I want to become
the joyful and obedient child You desire, walking in Your
way instead of pouting and protesting on the sidelines. In
Jesus' name, amen.

Day 345

JOYFUL MAKEOVER

*Blessed be the name of the Lord. . . . From the rising
of the sun to the going down of it. . .the name of
the Lord is to be praised! . . . [The Lord] raises the
poor out of the dust and lifts the needy from the ash
heap and the dung hill, that He may seat them with
princes. . . . He makes the barren woman to be a
homemaker and a joyful mother of [spiritual] children.*
PSALM 113:2–3, 7–9 AMPC

I want to not just praise You in the morning and evening,
Lord, but to praise You all the day long! To seek out the light
You send me to guide me throughout my day. To attend to
Your whispers, alert to Your promptings, changing my plans
to Yours. For You are the one who can raise the poorest of
souls into the richness of heaven. You are the one with the
plan so superior to mine. Where I have once seen a dead
end, a failed dream, a fading hope, You show me a new road,
a plan that succeeds, and a blazing path forward. You do far
more than my limited mind can even fathom. And in this I
find Your joy becomes mine! Thank You, Abba God! Amen!

LOVE REMINDERS

*But you, Lord, are a compassionate and gracious God,
slow to anger, abounding in love and faithfulness.*
PSALM 86:15 NIV

. . . .

Love is such an ambiguous, big, simple word. Yet, what it contains is the undercurrent of unconditionality. You love unconditionally. You love me when I mess up. You love me when I try and fail. I know this well. I see Your personal reminders in heart shapes in the cream of my coffee. I see leaves scattered underfoot in the shape of hearts. God, I see hearts in makeup splatters, cement designs, and spills.

All of these reminders draw me back to love. You are love. You love me. I am loved unconditionally. And even when my soul struggles to understand this, would You please echo this in front of my eyes and bring my heart to scripture and truth so that the constant messaging that I saturate in is love? Deep, simple, unconditional love. Amen.

Day 347

STRENGTH TO ENDURE

As you learn more and more how God works, you will learn how to do your work. We pray that you'll have the strength to stick it out over the long haul— not the grim strength of gritting your teeth but the glory-strength God gives. It is strength that endures the unendurable and spills over into joy, thanking the Father who makes us strong enough to take part in everything bright and beautiful that he has for us.
COLOSSIANS 1:10–12 MSG

. . . .

Just when I think I've had it, just when I think I can endure no more, just when my strength is gone, You bring me hope. You give me an infusion of strength and power. And suddenly my desperation has turned into joy! For You have kept me going, Lord! You have given me the strength to continue, to get to the place of beauty and joy, a place I never would have seen had I given up and dropped out! Thank You, Jesus, for giving me the faith and power to keep on keeping on until I reach all things bright and beautiful in You. Amen.

Day 348

LIVING AWAKE

For anything that becomes visible is light.
Therefore it says, "Awake, O sleeper, and arise
from the dead, and Christ will shine on you."
EPHESIANS 5:14 ESV

At church we read a prayer, and a few words connected to my soul: *open*, *empty*, *awake*. God, please help me live awake every day. Help me look for You in the details and people.

Where do You want me to live fully, with eyes open, palms out, and a heart surrendered to where Your Spirit is guiding and moving? God, where are You inviting me to live awake? Where am I sleepy or shut down?

God, I'm asking Your Spirit to gently pull back the covers and help me to my feet so that I may live awake. For when I live awake in Your Spirit, I live alive. And this is where You are glorified. So I ask: Where is Your attentive gaze drawing me to live awake? What does this look like today? Amen.

Day 349

LIVING THE LIFE!

Seize life! Eat bread with gusto, drink wine with a robust heart. Oh yes—God takes pleasure in your pleasure! Dress festively every morning. Don't skimp on colors and scarves. Relish life with the spouse you love each and every day of your precarious life. Each day is God's gift. It's all you get in exchange for the hard work of staying alive. Make the most of each one! Whatever turns up, grab it and do it. And heartily!
ECCLESIASTES 9:7–10 MSG

. . . .

Lord, I don't want to go through my day as if it's just one more in the line of many humdrum days that have gone before it. I want to *seize* this day! To live as if it might be my last. To enjoy all the things You have blessed me with—visible and invisible! I don't want a day to go by without telling the special people in my life that I love them, treasure them—and that includes You, Lord. You are my joy, my source, my ready and willing friend. And I love You more than I'd ever thought possible. Help me, Lord, to live this life to the full, in joy and with passion, making the most of all the opportunities You lay at my feet. Amen.

Day 350

GROWTH

*But grow in the grace and knowledge of our
Lord and Savior Jesus Christ. To him be the glory
both now and to the day of eternity. Amen.*
2 PETER 3:18 ESV

God, I notice that in order to grow, I have to put down something to pick up something new. With this comes grief. I grieve what no longer fits, what I'm outgrowing. Lord, would You please continue speaking to me about what needs to die so that my spirit can hold the new work You are doing?

What coping mechanisms, habits, or comforts are You inviting me to put down? Where are You inviting me into a new way of living? I apologize for beating myself up for feeling embarrassed for grieving what has died. I know this is necessary to heal, and I ask for healing and comfort where growth means death in some way.

I want to continue walking into hope. Hope is life. I don't want to neglect what I'm leaving behind, but to celebrate that it was beautiful for a season. Please remind me where I need to grieve what's been outgrown and step forward into growth. Amen.

Day 351

ECHOING THE WORD

When the Message we preached came to you, it wasn't just words. Something happened in you. The Holy Spirit put steel in your convictions. You paid careful attention to the way we lived among you, and determined to live that way yourselves. In imitating us, you imitated the Master. Although great trouble accompanied the Word, you were able to take great joy from the Holy Spirit!—taking the trouble with the joy, the joy with the trouble. . . . Your lives are echoing the Master's Word.
1 THESSALONIANS 1:5–6, 8 MSG

. . . .

Oh Lord, how wonderful this life is. Day after day, You demonstrate Your love for me. You have chosen me to do something special for You. That's why, when I read Your Word, I become so much a part of it and it becomes so much a part of me. For it prompts Your Spirit to move within me, helping me to live my life as Jesus lived His, to walk in His footsteps and love as He loved. It's to the point that, even though I may suffer at times, I still find my joy in You. Continue to make me and my life an echo of Your Word, from here to heaven and back. Amen.

Day 352

SLEEP IN HEAVENLY PEACE

Answer me when I call, O my God Who is right and good! You have made a way for me when I needed help. Be kind to me, and hear my prayer. . . . You have filled my heart with more happiness than they have when there is much grain and wine. I will lie down and sleep in peace. O Lord, You alone keep me safe.
PSALM 4:1, 7–8 NLV

. . . .

There are few things more precious than a good night's sleep. And that's just what I get when I put all my trust in You, Lord. When my head hits the pillow, before I know it, thoughts about the day echo in my mind. These thoughts are soon followed by what-ifs about tomorrow. But thinking about the future rarely helps me relax and fall asleep. Thus, when what-ifs approach, I allow them to pass me by. I begin thinking about how You continually pave a way for me to walk. How You lift me up and out of trouble—or walk with me through it. And that's all I need, to find You surrounding me, shielding me from harm. It is then I find my blessed peace. In Jesus' name, amen.

Day 353

A GOOD PLACE

I cried to the Lord in my trouble, and He. . .put me in a good place. The Lord is with me. I will not be afraid of what man can do to me. The Lord is with me. He is my Helper. . .my strength and my song. . .the One Who saves me. The joy of being saved is being heard in the tents of those who are right and good. The right hand of the Lord does powerful things.

PSALM 118:5–7, 14–15 NLV

. . . .

Lord, I cannot help but sing praises, to be filled with child-like joy! For when I cry out to You, You swoop down and lift me up. You put me in a good place, one where I can catch my breath, see things anew, regain my hope and strength. Because You are with me, I need not fear anything! For You are my helper, my strength, my song. Because Your Son has made me good and right in Your eyes, You will never let me fall. All day long, my joy, my courage, my blessings are met in the mantra, "You, Lord, are with me. You, Lord, are with me." In Jesus' name, amen.

Day 354

HAPPY IS SHE

The Lord says, "Hold on to what is right and fair.
Do what is right and good. My saving power will
soon come, and I will show what is right. How happy
is the man who does this, and the son of man who
takes hold of it! How happy is he who keeps the Day of
Rest holy, and keeps his hand from doing wrong."
ISAIAH 56:1–2 NLV

. . . .

This can be a crazy and mixed-up world, Lord. "Doing the right thing" seems to have gone out of style. But You, Lord, have told me what is right and wrong, fair and unfair. In fact, You have left Your Word for me as a guideline and Your Son, Jesus, as an example to follow. So I'm following Your guide and His example. For that is what brings me—and You—joy! Power me up with Your love, Lord, so I can live Your way. Prompt me to cease my work at times, so I can get the rest I need, be renewed in Your strength and light, and find the power to resist a world that wants me to go another way. I'm walking *Your* path, Lord, from here to eternity. In Jesus' name, amen.

Day 355

A NEW DAY

This is the day that the Lord has made. Let us be full of joy and be glad in it. O Lord, we beg You to save us! O Lord, we ask that You let everything go well for us! Great and honored is he who comes in the name of the Lord. We honor you from the house of the Lord. The Lord is God. He has given us light.

PSALM 118:24–27 NLV

. . . .

Good morning, Glory! I'm ready to rise and shine! For this is a new day, one You have made. You've set the sun in the sky, the moon in the shadows, and the stars behind Your heavenly blue. Today I am going to be full of joy—for You have brought me a clean slate, a new place to start. I have no idea of all the blessings You have waiting for me, but I am ready to begin by praising You. Today I will focus on all the good around me. I'll be keeping my eyes open to the opportunities that wait just around the corner. Shine Your light upon my path today, Lord. Give me success in all I do. And I will honor You every moment of this day as I walk Your way. Amen.

Day 356

JOY IN PRAYER

"As for the outsiders who now follow me, working for me, loving my name, and wanting to be my servants—all who keep Sabbath and don't defile it, holding fast to my covenant—I'll bring them to my holy mountain and give them joy in my house of prayer. They'll be welcome to worship the same as the 'insiders.' . . . My house of worship will be known as a house of prayer for all people."
ISAIAH 56:6–8 MSG

. . . .

When I first found You, Lord, I felt like an outsider. But as I learned more about You and spent more time in Your Word, I began to feel like an insider. I want to please You, to serve You in every way, shape, and form. I will rest as You bid me rest. Work as You bid me work. Love as You bid me love. Serve as You bid me serve. I thank You for loving me, wanting me, pulling me to You, and bringing me to Your holy mountain. As I enter into Your house, bringing my prayers and praises to You, lying down at Your feet, I will find the joy You so readily promise in that process. In Jesus' name, amen.

THE DOER OF GREAT THINGS

*When the Lord brought back the captives [who returned]
to Zion, we were like those who dream [it seemed so
unreal]. Then were our mouths filled with laughter,
and our tongues with singing. Then they said among
the nations, The Lord has done great things for them.
The Lord has done great things for us! We are glad!*
PSALM 126:1–3 AMPC

. . . .

I am amazed at the mercy You show me, Lord. The way
You keep standing with me, loving me, working in me. You
never give up. Just when I seem the most irredeemable,
You somehow redeem me. Just when I'm the most careless with my life, You take the most care of me. You have
said that You will never leave nor forsake me. That I can
never be taken out of Your hand. I thank You, Lord, for
that, for continually bringing me back to You, for doing
wonderful, awe-inspiring things for me. You are a dream
come true. You fill my mouth with laughter, my heart with
joy. And I, Father, am eternally grateful. In Jesus' name I
pray and say, amen.

Day 358

A HARBINGER OF LOVE

I always thank God when I speak of you in my prayers. It is because I hear of your love and trust in the Lord Jesus and in all the Christians. I pray that our faith together will help you know all the good things you have through Christ Jesus. Your love has given me much joy and comfort. The hearts of the Christians have been made happy by you.

PHILEMON 1:4–7 NLV

Lord, thank You for the love You have poured out upon me. Thank You for its power, how it can never be quenched (see Song of Solomon 8:7). How, even when compared with faith and hope, nothing is greater than love. Nothing—living or dead, from heaven or hell, from now or tomorrow, high or low, thinkable or unthinkable—can separate Your love from me. Show me in my life, Lord, whom I can love, care for, or comfort as an extension of Your love. For in doing so, I know I will be making another's burden lighter or another's day brighter. Help me, Lord, be a child of Your love, one who cannot help but share her joy of that love and so bring joy to someone else's heart. Amen.

Day 359

GOD'S RESTING PLACE

Let us go into His tabernacle; let us worship at His footstool. Arise, O Lord, to Your resting-place, You and the ark [the symbol] of Your strength. Let Your priests be clothed with righteousness (right living and right standing with God); and let Your saints shout for joy! . . . This is My resting-place forever [says the Lord]; here will I dwell, for I have desired it.
PSALM 132:7–9, 14 AMPC

. . . .

Out of all the places You could have chosen to live, Lord, You decided to live in me. It makes me reel in wonder that I, this fragile and flawed vessel, am where You reside. Your strength and power are within me. Through me, You can change the world, by little and great words and deeds. Keep me mindful of this reality, Lord. Help me to step aside so You can work, pouring out Your light and love. Show me the way You would have me direct my feet so that I am where You would have me be. I know You have a plan, Lord. And I am amazed and overjoyed that I am part of that plan. Help me rest in You as You rest in me. In Jesus' name I pray, amen.

Day 360

A SOFT HEART

*Christ (the Messiah) was faithful over His [own
Father's] house as a Son [and Master of it]. And it
is we who are [now members] of this house, if we
hold fast and firm to the end our joyful and exultant
confidence and sense of triumph in our hope [in
Christ]. Therefore, as the Holy Spirit says: Today,
if you will hear His voice, do not harden your hearts.*

HEBREWS 3:6–8 AMPC

I admit, Lord, that some days I may not be as open to
You as I should be. I'm so focused on getting through my
earthly tasks that I forget about my heavenly mission. Or
I hear Your voice but harden my heart against it. I brush
it aside, figuring that if I have time later in my day, then
I'll respond to what You would have me say or do. At
other times, Lord, fear keeps me from going down the
path You'd have me trod. So help me to have an eager ear
and a soft heart where You are concerned, Lord. To hold
fast to my hope and expectation of Jesus in this life and
beyond. Give me the will, means, courage, and openness
to joyfully do what You desire, no matter when and no
matter how. Amen.

RENEWAL

Turn to freedom our captivity and restore our fortunes,
O Lord, as the streams in the South (the Negeb) [are
restored by the torrents]. They who sow in tears shall
reap in joy and singing. He who goes forth bearing
seed and weeping [at needing his precious supply
of grain for sowing] shall doubtless come again
with rejoicing, bringing his sheaves with him.

PSALM 126:4–6 AMPC

. . . .

Only You, Lord, can turn my life around. Only You can make me free again. Only You can restore what I once was or had. So I ask You to do that today, Lord. Turn my tears of sorrow into tears of joy. Remind me of all You have done in my life in the past, all the miracles You have worked, all the ways You have spoken into my heart. I am in need of Your comfort, Lord. I long for the joy I once had. I'm reaching out for the love that has saved me, bringing me back from the brink time and time again. Your having renewed me in the past gives me so much hope in this present moment. I'm already feeling the light of Your presence breaking through my clouds of sorrow. Lift me up with You, Lord, as I rejoice in You anew! Amen.

Day 362

RISE AND SHINE!

Arise [from the depression and prostration in which
circumstances have kept you—rise to a new life]!
Shine (be radiant with the glory of the Lord), for
your light has come, and the glory of the Lord has
risen upon you! For behold, darkness shall cover
the earth, and dense darkness [all] peoples, but the
Lord shall arise upon you. . .and His glory shall be
seen on you. And nations shall come to your light.
ISAIAH 60:1–3 AMPC

. . . .

Some days, Lord, I find myself so weighed down by life, by circumstances, and by the world around me that I find it hard to get out of bed. I just want to bury myself beneath the covers and wait for the tide to turn. That's when I realize I'm losing sight of Your light, Your command to rise and shine. So enter into me in a powerful way today, Lord. Fill me with the glory of Your light. Renew my faith. Pull me back into the right reality—Your reality—Your world of joy, love, power, gladness, and thanksgiving. Come to me, Lord. Brighten my spirit so I can once more be glad and reflect the light of Your Son! In His name, amen.

Day 363

JOY ALONG THE WAY

Let us put every thing out of our lives that keeps us from doing what we should. Let us keep running in the race that God has planned for us. Let us keep looking to Jesus. Our faith comes from Him and He is the One Who makes it perfect. He did not give up when He had to suffer shame and die on a cross. He knew of the joy that would be His later. Now He is sitting at the right side of God.
HEBREWS 12:1–2 NLV

. . . .

God, I don't want to give up as I travel with You through this amazing journey called the way. So help me get rid of anything in my life that keeps me from doing what Your Word would have me do. Help me keep going on this path You have carved out for me. Help me to keep my focus on Jesus and not the winds of adversity. For He is the one who keeps me going, who has the power over all things and makes my path straight, right, and good. Just as He suffered to get to the joy that was His, help me to keep going, knowing that I too will one day be in heaven, rejoicing with Him! Amen.

BIG AND SMALL

In the day when I called, You answered me; and You strengthened me with strength (might and inflexibility to temptation) in my inner self. . . . Sing of the ways of the Lord and joyfully celebrate His mighty acts, for great is the glory of the Lord. For though the Lord is high, yet has He respect to the lowly [bringing them into fellowship with Him]. . . . Though I walk in the midst of trouble, You will revive me; You will stretch forth Your hand.

PSALM 138:3, 5–7 AMPC

It's almost unfathomable, unimaginable, Lord, that You, who created the world and hold such power, love, and the destiny of one and all, take notice of me. My life is just a blip on Your map of eternity. Yet You care about me and everything that's happening in my life. So continue to answer my pleas and prayers, Lord. Strengthen me with all the might I need—within and without. Revive me amid troubles, big and small. Stretch forth Your hand to help. Hold me as I sing with joy about all that You have done, will do, and are doing in me! Amen.

Day 365

HEALING SUN

*Prove Me now by it, says the Lord of hosts, if I
will not open the windows of heaven for you and
pour you out a blessing, that there shall not be
room enough to receive it. . . . Unto you who revere
and worshipfully fear My name shall the Sun of
Righteousness arise with healing in His wings and
His beams, and you shall go forth and gambol like
calves [released] from the stall and leap for joy.*
MALACHI 3:10; 4:2 AMPC

. . . .

When I give my all to You, Lord, You return to me so much
more. Your blessings are so many and so massive that I
cannot hold them all. On top of all this, You have allowed
Your Son to die for me. When I am basking in His presence,
worshipping and loving Him, He rises up and heals me. He
takes all my sin stains and makes them white as snow. He
takes all my prayers and turns them into praises. He takes
all my sorrows and replaces them with joy. Thank You,
Lord, for all You have allowed so that I can dance, sing,
and leap for joy in the "Son-shine." In Jesus' name, amen.

SCRIPTURE INDEX